Pathways to Union with Jesus

Pathways to
Union *with* Jesus

William Wilson

XULON PRESS

Xulon Press
555 Winderley Pl, Suite 225
Maitland, FL 32751
407.339.4217
www.xulonpress.com

© 2024 by William Wilson

All rights reserved solely by the author. The author guarantees all contents are original and do not infringe upon the legal rights of any other person or work. No part of this book may be reproduced in any form without the permission of the author.

Due to the changing nature of the Internet, if there are any web addresses, links, or URLs included in this manuscript, these may have been altered and may no longer be accessible. The views and opinions shared in this book belong solely to the author and do not necessarily reflect those of the publisher. The publisher therefore disclaims responsibility for the views or opinions expressed within the work.

Unless otherwise indicated, Scripture quotations taken from the Holy Bible, New International Version (NIV). Copyright © 1973, 1978, 1984, 2011 by Biblica, Inc.™. Used by permission. All rights reserved.

Paperback ISBN-13: 979-8-86850-508-9
Ebook ISBN-13: 979-8-86850-509-6

THE FULFILLMENT OF A PERSON'S LIFE IS UNION WITH JESUS IN LOVE

"Grace be with all who love our Lord Jesus Christ with love incorruptible." Eph 6:24

CONTENTS

Introduction: The Simple And Supreme Act Of
                Loving Faith In Christ. ix

Preliminaries: Grace, Works, And Forgivenss . . xix

Chapter One: Destination of the Pathways Purity
                Of Heart: 1

Chapter Two: The Pathway Of Lectio Divina . . . 29

Chapter Three: The Pathway Of The
                Jesus Prayer 85

Chapter Four: The Pathway Of Discernment
                Of Thought 113

Chapter Five: The Pathway Of Spiritual
                Direction 147

Chapter Six: The Pathway Of Life 197

INTRODUCTION
THE SIMPLE AND SUPREME ACT OF LOVING FAITH IN JESUS

My Journey

Our chaotic experience in life in this world makes us seek an explanation, meaning, and purpose. Jesus is the answer, but at birth we do not know Him. Somewhere along life's road, Jesus appears to us. Those who are willing to receive Him begin to live, truly live, for the first time with understanding and known destiny in the world.

I grew up in a non-religious household. Both parents were alcoholic. Estranged from each other they found solace in passing relationships with other mates. We lived in squalid poverty in the Kensington section of Northeast Philadelphia. My socialization took place on the streets in a corner gang where

I also learned, very badly, about sex. Kensington was a vast society of people stuck in grinding poverty, many using alcohol as an analgesic and sex as a palliative recreation. A few found meaning and hope in religion.

Teen-age mental confusion, emotional depression, and moral guilt and shame led me into a year-long struggle with strong suicidal aspirations. At seventeen I turned to God in repentance and was morally strengthened by a few new good friends. The affection of a sweet and innocent high-school girl from a better family and neighborhood brought me to new life and hope. By working a day shift and a part time night job during the summer I raised enough money to at least start college at the University of Pennsylvania. In my freshman year, I began to be visited by powerful impressions of God. At times, I felt overcome with desire for God.

At the end of freshman year, I entered New Melleray Abbey near Dubuque Iowa, a Cistercian-Trappist monastery in the Benedictine tradition of the Roman Catholic Church. It was a thousand miles from my home, physically and figuratively. It was a tough change for a recently converted street kid. The silence was absolute. No visitors were allowed. No leaving the cloister. No contact of any kind with the

Pathways to Union with Jesus

outside world. It was an austere life of fasting, abstinence, and renunciation of the world under the vows of poverty, celibacy, and obedience. Some novices had mental breakdowns. I barely survived the first six years; then I began to flourish. What made the difference was the discovery, the practice, and the fruits of contemplative prayer.

Let me be more specific. In the monastery we had no communication because of the rule of perpetual silence and cut off human interaction by physical restriction to the cloister. We had no access to newspapers, radio, TV, or telephone. There was no recreation. We ate only vegetables, slept on hay-covered boards, and fasted on one full meal a day during most of the year. We worked in silence in the fields, barns, and workshops. I lost weight. In Iowa, winter weather is long, starting in October and lasting until May. Every winter day I felt cold and nauseous from rising at 3:15 a.m. until we ate our one full meal at noon. It was a very austere life.

One winter day as I walked in the line of silent hooded monks toward the refectory for the noon meal, I cried out to God in my heart: "Lord Jesus, only if you make me know your love can I endure this life! But Lord, if you do not show me your love, I cannot endure this life." He did show me His love and I stayed for 25 years. Without the blessings of the Pathways I am handing on to you, I would not have survived, much less thrived in the penitential monastic life. Monastic austerity can rightly be criticized. Nevertheless, one indisputable advantage of monastic life is that it creates a regular, simple, quiet, solitary lifestyle that a Christian can use to maximize personal communion with God.

After eleven years in the monastery, I was given permission to retire to a tiny one-room cabin in the woods to live as a solitary hermit monk. Of course, there was no electricity or plumbing. After seven years in that solitude, I was appointed chaplain (spiritual director, priest, confessor, and teacher) for the nuns in our Trappistine Convent of Mississippi Abbey. Some years later I was promoted to Formation Director of the young monks at New Melleray. At age 44, I entered upon a decade of frontier missionary work in the Bolivian Andes, which developed into Amistad Mission. At 51, I married a medical missionary, Dr. Susan Winchester. By age 61 we had two children. After returning to the United States, I served as chaplain, first in a retirement community and later in a maximum-security prison. I taught spirituality to graduate students at Drew University Seminary and gave spiritual retreats around the United States and abroad. I rose to senior associate

Pathways to Union with Jesus

Rector in a prominent parish and subsequently became a missionary bishop in the Anglican Church.

From my origins in the hood, I now live in undeserved social honor and material privilege. Yet, my experience and prayer remain the same: "Lord Jesus, only if you make me know your love can I endure this life!" He does. And I continue to thrive. I wrote this book to instruct and encourage you, my brothers and sisters, in the ways of looking on Jesus with loving faith so that you too will not just survive but thrive in your walk through the arduous pathway of life.

This Book

This book presents the most important ways of seeking transforming union with Jesus. It is an invitation to the uninitiated to begin seeking Jesus and an encouragement to seekers to intensify their quest. These personal devotions should be integrated within a full life of active membership in a Christian community of faith, love, and worship. They will enrich a person's life in a church community but they will not substitute for it.

Sources: After the Holy Bible, I learned the spiritual and ascetical teachings presented here from the Christian monastic and mystical literary tradition, from St. Anthony (+356) and the Desert Fathers down to Thomas Merton and Richard Foster in our generation.

Overview: After this Introduction, the Prelims explain how we can think about the mystery of Grace and Works and then issues a Call to Forgive, because without forgiveness there can be no spiritual growth. The first chapter identifies and describes the subjective destination of the Pathways as the state of Purity of Heart. Chapters two through five present detailed explanations of four perennial streams of orthodox Christian spirituality: Lection Divine, The Jesus Prayer, Discernment of Thoughts, and Spiritual Direction. The final chapter, The Pathway of Life, encourages readers to seek and find union with Jesus in all of their experiences in life.

Purpose

A potential problem facing the beginner on the spiritual journey is confusion caused by the bewildering variety of pathways, old and new, presented in an endless profusion of books, courses, and teachers of spiritual practice. I composed this writing to guide the seeker into the heart of the classical tradition of Christian spirituality. I received the four great essential disciplines at the heart of this book from our ancient forerunners in the pathways of Christian spirituality. Now it is my privilege to pass them on to you.

During the long course of the history of Christian spirituality, it is natural for emphasis and nomenclature to vary with the centuries and cultures. However, it is unquestionably certain that in every age anyone seeking to grow in transforming union with God in Jesus Christ will need to: (1) communicate with God through God's Word (Lectio Divina); (2) seek increasing personal intimacy with the Person of the Risen Lord (The Jesus Prayer); (3) be transformed by renewal of their mind (Discernment of Thoughts); and (4) have the protection and confirmation of the church in the person of at least one other Christian spiritual companion (Spiritual Direction).

To the objective validation from the antiquity and universality of these four devotional practices, I humbly add my own personal testimony. I have carried out these four devotions (very imperfectly!) during the fifty-five years of my adult life. They have empowered me to overcome the inauspicious circumstances of severe poverty and a dysfunctional alcoholic family in my childhood. Over the decades, they have protected me from disastrous errors of excess and defect in my thinking and in my action. They have enabled me to become a world-affirming Christian contemplative. These four pathways not only saved my life, they have also led me to increasing union with God in Jesus; and that union has brought me serendipitous joy, richness of love relationships and wonderfully fruitful ministries of compassion in the world.

The Spirit has completely convinced me that the value of everything that transpires within the individual human heart, and the excellence of every human word and deed, flow from our spiritual union with Jesus Christ. The sufferings of life are too great to bear without the strength, comfort and hope that come from knowing Jesus in contemplative prayer. On biblical faith and personal experience, I declare that only by the power of life-giving union with Jesus can you, I, or anyone else, achieve his or her highest potential in wisdom, creativity, and relationships of love in the world. I pray and I promise that your practice of these four disciplines of Christian spirituality will progressively deepen your union with Jesus.

It is impossible that this book could be an easy read. Its subject matter is metaphysical and mystical: spiritual discipline and the mystery of transforming union with Jesus. The teaching will challenge your mind and the practice will stretch your will. But the fruit is worth the labor. As far as the writer and the reader are led by the Spirit of God, this book can become the occasion of grace that will enrich your life forever. Be prepared for hard work and for even greater blessing! Expect to be transformed by these devotional disciplines that all converge in the simple and supreme act of loving faith in Jesus.

PRELIMINARIES:
GRACE, WORKS AND FORGIVENESS

Before embarking upon the pathways, it is of the uttermost importance for the traveler to understand that Christians renounce every form of 'works spirituality'. We live by God's grace. We are not at all passive. Rather we are passionate in seeking fulfillment in a spiritual union with God. Yet we always live in the awareness that we seek only because we are being drawn by God. Divine grace is the source of our efforts.

The relationship between divine grace and human effort is implicit on many pages of this book. It seems advisable, therefore, to clarify our understanding of this mystery now at the beginning.

GRACE AND WORKS

Informed by biblical revelation, Christians believe that God will judge all human beings on their works. "For we must all appear before the judgment seat of Christ, so that each one may receive what is due for what he has done in the body, whether good or evil." (2Cor 5:10) God "will render to each one according to his works". (Rm 2:6)

Paradoxically, Christians also believe that God's love for us, and all of the gifts that come to us from His love, are pure gifts of His grace, absolutely independent of our works. We are "justified by His grace as a gift". Paul tells us that those who believe are "chosen by grace. But if it is by grace it is on longer on the basis of works, otherwise grace would no longer be grace." (Rm11:5-6)

In your life and in this book, you will often be told that all that is good in us and all the good we do comes not from us but from Christ in us. You will also often be told to work, to strive heroically, to desire, think, speak, and do good things. How can we understand this seeming contradiction?

In the very essence of our created being, we human beings are *freely responsive.* The initiative belongs to God. We cannot bring forth our own existence. God speaks the creative word and we respond by coming into being.

A human person is a capacity to be lived by God. We are the activity of God Who holds us in existence by His Word. The person He holds in existence is a free agent who can accept or decline the gifts of God. Before we have one good desire, one sincere prayer, one compassionate thought toward another, etc, God presents it to our freedom. We freely choose to allow God to give us a good desire, a generous action, a humble prayer. Sometimes we do not allow the Spirit to live in us. We refuse the gift of His Life in us. We choose to live in the alienated isolated false self, with its selfish desires, words, and actions.

Every good thought, desire, word, or work of ours is Christ living in us. All of the true and beautiful thoughts of goodness and love that arise within us, every word of truth and deed of love –all are first God's gifts to us. When we freely receive them they become our life and it is no longer just we who live but Christ is living in us.

Dear Ones, if I were to lay upon you a book full of works for you to accomplish merely by your effort and will power, I would be cursing you and acting as antichrist in your life. God mercifully forbid! Please understand: every "let us", "must", "ought" and "should" that you read in this book is only an invitation for you to freely choose to ask and receive some gift of God. All of our good works, from the least holy desire to the greatest fruit of sacrificial love, are all God's gifts of Life to us. With this understanding of how grace works, it is safe for me to proceed in this book to stir your desire and prayer for God's gifts of spiritual discipline.

FORGIVENESS

Personal and pastoral experience has taught me that the lack of forgiveness is the most frequent impediment to growth in the spiritual life. There can be no growth in the spiritual life of union with Jesus without forgiveness. The disciplines urged in these pages cannot produce good fruit in anyone who does not receive God's forgiveness and forgive those who offend them. For this reason, before going further, I ask any readers who are living in unforgiveness to pause here and walk with me through the cleansing act of forgiveness. Forgiving follows being forgiven.

First: Be Forgiven

One of the most profound summary statements of the whole Gospel of Christ is this: 'Your sins are forgiven.' Christ's death on the cross brought God's forgiveness of all sins of all people of all time. Period! However, God's forgiveness makes no difference in the life of the forgiven person unless he or she believes and receives it.

Scripture urges us to confess our sins to one another. (Js 5:16) Confession to a sister or brother has a cathartic healing effect. The human compassion and forgiveness we receive from the Christian in whom we confide is a sign, a sacrament, of the mercy and pardon God gives to us. Confession of sin is a humbling act of truth. Paradoxically, this truthful humiliation before a fellow Christian relieves us of shame. Repentance can be a secret conversation between God and the penitent. However, when our repentance becomes visible in the world, even to just one person to whom we confess, it becomes a blessing that would not happen if our repentance were kept a secret to God alone. Love requires us to ask forgiveness of anyone whom we have personally offended. Yet, in case of secret personal sin, spiritual discretion and the danger of scandal could be good reasons why we would not divulge our sin to another human being but only to God.

Nothing we do or fail to do prevents our compassionate God from forgiving us. However, there are two mistakes we can make that will prevent us from *receiving* God's forgiveness: refusing to believe in His forgiveness and refusing to acknowledge our sins. To correct the first, all we need to do now is decide in our hearts to believe in the atoning blood of Jesus shed on the cross for the forgiveness of the sins of the world, including all of mine. If we have not done so before, do it right now. Be sure you understand that God's forgiveness extends to *all* of your sins of all of your life, no matter how gross or trivial they are. You are completely forgiven of all of your sins by your complete reception of His forgiveness. Amen.

The second error that can prevent us from receiving forgiveness from God is failure to acknowledge our sins. If our confession to another person would scandalize him or her, we should at least acknowledge our sin before God. God, the Reader of Hearts, hears our secret confession.

Sins that we do not acknowledge remain unforgiven –not unforgiven by God, but by ourselves. We do not ask for forgiveness of sins that we do not

Pathways to Union with Jesus

recognize as sins. They remain as accepted parts of our lives. And they wreak havoc in our souls and in our relationships. Every sin against God and others is also a sin against ourselves. Our personal sins ruin our lives more than any enemy ever could. We must become aware of such sins so that we can place them under the atoning Blood for God's forgiveness… and then we must forgive ourselves.

Here we encounter a problem: Our false ego-self is in a constant state of denial concerning anything that is wrong with our behavior. In our ego blindness, we do not let ourselves see the log in our own eye! Our "heart is deceitful above all things and desperately sick: who can understand it?" (Jer 17:9) Sins in our conscious awareness are all we can see, like the tip of an iceberg. There is far more beneath the surface of our consciousness.

There are two things we can do to combat our moral blindness. We can converse with our own souls in an effort to convince ourselves that willingness to become aware of our unconscious sins is the doorway to a happier life and more fulfilling relationships with others. And more importantly, we can pray. We can ask God to reveal our hidden sins that we may confess them and be freed from their hold on our lives. Following the example of David, we pray:

Lord, "Who can discern his errors? Declare me innocent from hidden faults." (Ps 19:12)

Once we have accepted God's forgiveness, we must not allow any self-doubts to linger in our hearts. After confession, leave no room for any vague sense of unworthiness, residual feelings of guilt, shame, or any other impression of "not being quite right" with God. All these self-denigrating feelings are all demonic lies. If you believe them, they will impede you from being filled with all the fullness of God in union with Jesus. You are forgiven. Now in full awareness, celebrate the joy of your blessed union in love with God in Christ. Then, having freely received the love of God that forgives you, freely we forgive others in love.

Second: Be Forgiving

To forgive means to accept the Blood of Jesus shed on the cross as payment in full for the sins and debts of others to you. Our blessed Lord Jesus shed His Blood on the cross as payment so that you would receive infinitely more than you lost from every sin ever committed against you. Your compassionate Father knows how much you have suffered from the sins of men. He makes it up to you a thousand times over by giving you His grace, eternal life, and divine glory in union with Jesus forever and ever.

Pathways to Union with Jesus

Our blessed Lord Jesus came from heaven to earth "to give knowledge of salvation to his people in the forgiveness of their sins". (Lk 1:77) Once we have heard the good news that our sins are forgiven in heaven, we are inspired to forgive others their sins against us. Indeed, we are absolutely bound to so, or else "neither will your Father forgive your trespasses." (Mt 6:15)

Jesus told us a parable about a king who forgave an enormous debt of one of his servants who went out and refused to forgive a petty debt of a fellow servant. It ends with the King refusing to forgive the wicked servant's debt. (Mt 18:23-35) In the Lord's Prayer we ask for forgiveness "as we also have forgiven our debtors" (Mt 6: 12). Both the unforgiving servant in the parable of Mt 18 and the Christian who prays the Lord's Prayer of Mt 6 *has already received forgiveness.* Just as we love because He first loved us, so we forgive because He first forgave us. Refusal to forgive others *after* receiving forgiveness from God is a grave sin. Remember: no one receives God's forgiveness for unconfessed sin. Until we confess our own sin of unforgiveness, we cannot receive forgiveness of it.

In Mathew 5:23, Jesus forbids us to go into God's presence in prayer until we have first forgiven and sought forgiveness from our brother or sister whom we have offended. Jesus says: "leave your gift there before the altar and go, first be reconciled." If your brother refuses to forgive you, that will be painful for you, but from that moment, you are at peace with God because you have done all that you can to reconcile. Now you are the offended person and you must forgive, even if the offending person does not admit doing wrong to you by his unforgiveness.

To "forgive your brother from your heart" (Mt 18:35) produces two essential fruit, both of which all of us can do, with the help of God's grace. (1) A forgiving person decides not to return evil to the offender (neither in thoughts, words, or deeds) and (2) he chooses to pray for the offender, asking for all of God's grace and mercy upon him or her.

True forgiveness does not require you to like the offender. You do not have to, nor should you, allow the offender to harm you again. Forgiving does not mean excusing or dismissing the evil things the offender has done to you. A deeply wounded person who truly forgives may go on feeling hurt, anger, and disgust toward the offender for a very long time. Emotional wounds need and deserve a long time to heal. For the sake of inner peace the wounded person should pray to be relieved of those unpleasant feelings. Spiritual forgiveness by choice is the necessary prerequisite for the emotional forgiveness that will eventually follow. The point is that we can choose to forgive even if we cannot change our negative feelings. The choice not to repay the evil in any way and to pray for the salvation of the offender constitutes complete theological and spiritual forgiveness, regardless of how we feel toward the offender.

If you have any doubt whether you are harboring any unforgiveness, do this: Look back on your life from your infancy to this day. Recall the person or persons, one at a time, who has wounded you. See each one in your imagination. Name their sin against you, however painful the memory may be. Then declare your faith in words like: "As I receive the total forgiveness of all my sins through the shed Blood of Jesus, I now receive the shed Blood of Jesus as payment in full for the debt owed to me by those who have harmed me." Now, in the greatness of your graced spirit, declare you decision not to return evil for the evil done to you, not even in an unkind thought. As you review the offenders, one by one, ask God to bless him or her even as God blesses you. For each offender, express your forgiveness prayer in your own words. Or you can use a prayer form like the following as your act of forgiveness of those who have offended you.

My Father in Heaven,

As You have forgiven me, so I want to forgive others. Father, I have been deeply wounded by …(name). But now, I receive the shed Blood of Jesus as payment in full for all of the failures and bad things (name) has done to me. In obedience to Jesus and following His example, I forgive (name) completely. I promise You, Holy Father, I will not deliberately think, speak, or do anything evil to…(name). Instead, I come to You, Abba Father, on behalf of …(name) and I ask You to grant (him or her) all the fullness of Your grace and blessing in this life and eternal happiness in the life to come. I ask this in the Name of Your Son Jesus Christ Our Lord. Amen.

You have now forgiven those who have offended you. You are free. Go on without impediment to seek deeper union with God in Jesus and to grow in your spiritual life, using the ancient traditions this book will pass on to you.

9/19/15

CHAPTER ONE

DESTINATION OF THE PATHWAYS PURITY OF HEART

DESTINATION: PURITY OF HEART

This is a book of instructions about how to engage in the four chief devotional practices of the Christian spiritual life. These ancient traditions are reliable pathways to transforming union with Jesus. Engagement in these devotions increasingly produces the state of spiritual maturity named, Purity of Heart. Purity of heart is not an activity. It is a habitual attitude, a permanent disposition, and an abiding quality of the way we live, think, feel, and respond in the world. A pure heart is tranquil, peaceful, content, confident, universally compassionate and beautiful in simplicity and humility.

When we set out on a road trip, the first thing we have to do is set the destination, perhaps by entering it into our GPS. Then the GPS calculates the directions, turn by turn. In our Christian walk, we are on a journey. Our eternal destination is union with Jesus in glory. Our temporal destination is union with Jesus by grace. We receive grace in the measure of the purity of our heart. The devotional practices this book teaches are the turn-by-turn directions to purity of heart.

Why is purity of heart so important? Because purity of heart is the necessary spiritual condition that enables us to be see Jesus and God in Him. Seeing Jesus in the vision of faith increases our love; love unites us with Jesus; union with Jesus transforms us into His likeness.

If the Lord Jesus were to stand directly in front of a woman, she would not be able to see Him unless she has purity of heart. Even if our Blessed Savior throws His arms around a person and presses her or him close to His bosom with uttermost loving tenderness, that person will not feel it if he or she does not have purity of heart. When our divine Lord Jesus manifests Himself, He is seen *only* by the pure of heart. Purity of heart begins with repentance: We turn away from sin and turn toward Jesus. As purity of heart increases, the Christian is transformed by knowing the love of Christ that surpasses knowledge. (Cf. Eph 3:19)

PURITY OF HEART

The Teaching Jesus Gave Us

"Blessed are the pure in heart, for they shall see God." In calling the pure in heart "blessed", our Lord declares that they have all of the grace, blessing, and beatitude that God has to give.

The Pure In Heart

The nine beatitudes of Mt 5 are parallel descriptions of the same person who has been reborn by grace. The pure in heart are *poor in spirit*, which means they know their need for God and trust in God for absolutely everything. These are people who *mourn* because they feel their own and others' sorrow for not yet having attained the fullness of the glory of God, which is the only true final happiness for which we all were made. These blessed *meek* feel no impulse to fight for the material good things of this temporal world. The riches of this world have become trivial to them because of the surpassing worth of the eternal divine treasure they already possess in their pure hearts. The pure in heart are sinners who hunger and thirst for the righteousness they receive through their faith in Christ. That very gift stirs in them an even greater *hunger and thirst for the complete righteousness* that consists in loving God and loving all other creatures with perfect love.

When the pure in heart fall into sin, they take flight into God's mercy. When they see another person suffering the sickness of sin, they have no condemnation but only commend them to the same Mercy in prayer. Living by the mercy of God, they are merciful to others.

Pure hearts are *peacemakers.* They forgive those who sin against them. They forgive every human being for every unkind deed, word, and even thought leveled against them. By their forgiveness the pure in heart attain peace for themselves and make peace with others.

When the pure in heart display these traits in their behavior, they are dearly loved by others of pure heart. But they are also virulently hated and *persecuted because of their righteousness* by the many whose hearts are not pure.

They Shall See God

In the natural human condition, no one can see or know God. We cannot hear sound waves beyond the audible range. Analogously, our power to know existing things is limited to a range of finite material beings. As mere humans, we simply cannot know God. By divine revelation, believers know that God always intended for us to be raised from our natural condition to the supernatural condition of participating in the divine nature. There are two stages in our elevation to supernatural life: the life of grace in time and the life of glory in eternity.

Only God can know God. God's gives us a supernatural revelation of Christ. When God's revelation is received by our faith, we know God in the Lord Jesus. Faith is not an opinion; it is not a feeling; it is certainly not a logical conclusion. *Faith is a personal experience of being illumined by God.* During our life and mission in time, our knowledge of God is indirect, mediated dimly as reflected in the mirror of our faith. Knowledge of God by faith is real but very imperfect. Purifying our heart enables the Christian to know God more truly and clearly...as though by cleansing the mirror of our faith.

In the Life to come, we will receive a divine power to see God face to face. Faith will come to an end when we have direct immediate vision. That higher power to know God directly is what Christians call the "Light of Glory". We are destined to this glory. Without purity of heart, no one shall see God in eternal glory.

Knowing God By Faith

The supernatural gift of faith becomes manifest to us when we become conscious in our personal spirit that we trust in Jesus for deliverance from all evil and for eternal life –eternal life now in our spirit and later in our body at the resurrection. The promise of

Pathways to Union with Jesus

heaven and the fear of hell do not coerce anyone to trust in Jesus. Nobody 'must' believe in Jesus because of some irrefragable rational argument. Why, then, do we believe? We believe because we have the undeniable experience of being drawn to Jesus Christ by God the Father through the Holy Spirit. Our experience of *being drawn* makes us know the One Who draws us and the One to Whom we are drawn. This is what it means to "see God" in this life. This is the indirect vision of faith.

Knowing is a kind of non-ocular seeing. We often say, " I see" when we mean that we understand what someone is explaining to us. This is a mental act of understanding or 'seeing' with the mind. This is a thinking activity of one's mind, *not* a knowing activity of one's personal spirit. We think with our mind. We know with our spirit.

Here is a simple analogy I use to convey what it means to know God in one's spirit by the personal experience of faith. Imagine a completely dark room. Two friends are there, but each thinks he is alone. Then one of them speaks and the other recognizes the voice of his friend and answers back. Following the sound, they find each other in the pitch dark. Hands clasp hands. They *know* each other in the dark. We live in this dark world. We hear the voice of the unseen One Who loves us. We run to Him and He to us. We feel the embrace of His love in our hearts. We know Him by experiencing Him in the dark during our life in time. We see Him in our spirit, but indirectly and dimly by faith, as if in a reflection from an ancient mirror of polished brass. When we pass from this world of time into eternity faith will pass away because we will receive the divine power to see Him as He is, Face to Face, in the Light of Glory.

We are not just pilgrims and exiles while we are on the earth. We are missionaries of Christ. He sent us into the world as the Father sent Him. As long as we live in this world we are on a twofold journey: to inner transformation and to outer fruitfulness in deeds of love. We will be inwardly transformed into Christ's likeness by abiding in Him Who lives in our hearts. We abide in Him by the prayer of loving attention. By faith we can gaze upon the face of Jesus Who dwells in our personal spirit. Seeing Him by faith with the eyes of our hearts enflames our love for Him. Loving Jesus transforms us in His likeness. The more we become inwardly like Jesus, the more fruitful we become in our outer life of sacrificial love in the world.

This is the supreme importance of purity of heart: it will enable us to know God in heaven in the vision of glory and it enables us to know God on earth in the vision of faith. This is eternal life, to know God and Jesus Christ Whom He has sent. Therefore, let us agree to desire, to pray, and to strive to become pure in heart.

Purity of Heart Through Discernment Of Thoughts

"Out of the heart come evil thoughts…" (Mt 15:19) Our Blessed Lord Jesus teaches us in this place that every evil word or deed that takes place in the visible material world proceeds from an invisible choice that has already been made in the heart. To make the fruit of our moral behavior good, we must first make the tree good, that is, we must have purity in our hearts in order to have purity in our actions. Purity of heart is the root, the only root, of all beautiful words and deeds of love.

"The Sower sows the Word…" (Mk 4:14) Here our dear Savior tells us that God is the origin of all good impulses: God the Father Sows the Word. Jesus is the Word of God Who includes in Himself

Pathways to Union with Jesus

all good and true, thoughts, feelings, words, and impulses of love.

Our Divine Lover does not force us to anything. He inspires, encourages, appeals, elicits, and empowers us to think and to do all good things. He sows every impulse that expresses His truth and love. Once sown in our hearts by the Spirit of God, it then pertains to each person to recognize and to receive the empowering word of love. Sometimes, we let the seed lay on the surface of our awareness, or we give it no attention…and that gives Satan opportunity to devour it through our forgetfulness before it bears the fruit of love in the world.

The first principle of discernment of thoughts is to be *vigilant*, looking out like a watchman to see the Sower of good thoughts in our hearts. As soon as we recognize that God is the Sower, we will cease upon the thoughts sown, love them, live them, and give thanks to God. God gives us both the thought and the accomplishment of the good impulses He sows in our hearts.

"While men were sleeping, his enemy came and sowed weeds among the wheat…" (Mt 13: 25) Our enemy is the enemy of God, Satan. Demons cast the evil thoughts/impulses that come into our mind and invite us to accept them. It is our responsibility to stay awake and discern the seed-thoughts that are sown in our hearts. Evil thoughts sown by the Enemy in our hearts have only the power of suggestion and deceitful allure. By the power of the Holy Spirit in us, we can recognize the deceitful, unloving, thoughts and refuse to agree with them. Finally, after denouncing the evil seed of the Enemy, wise Christians pray, asking the Lord Jesus to "deliver us from the Evil One". His answer is not only "Yes"; He would even die on a cross to answer that prayer!

"For all that is in the world [is] the desires of the flesh, the desires of the eyes, and the pride of life." (1Jn 2:16) Christians are sent into this world to bring light, love, and truth into it. Therefore we must not become part of the world while we are in the world. Christians engage in unobjectionable secular activities of this world such as commerce, recreation, sports etc, but we do so in a manner that subordinates them to our life in the Spirit. We "deal with the world as though they had no dealings with it". (1Cor 7:31).

Let each one examine her or his own conduct. Do I spend too much time involved with the conversation, values, and interests of this world, beyond what is required by my mission in the world?

Pathways to Union with Jesus

If you are a spouse, a parent, a doctor, lawyer, teacher, soldier, plumber, gardener, farmer, or whatever else: Be the best you can be! For God's glory, for the benefit of those you serve in love, and for your own fulfillment in life, whatever you do, do it as well as you possibly can, empowered by the Almighty Spirit of the Resurrection. Beyond that, guard your mind for thinking the thoughts of God. For this purpose, do not squander too much of your free time staring at digital screens, social media, T V talking heads, and other 'empty' entertainments. By all means, have fun, relax, and enjoy. Just do not let the Christian values of fun and recreation deteriorate into wasting your mind and heart in pursuit of the false values and vain interests of this unbelieving world.

Seek the love of Jesus. In both senses: seek to know His personal love for you and seek to increase your love for Him. Nothing will help you more in your search for intimacy with Jesus than reading, praying, and meditating, on the four Gospels and devoutly receiving the mystery of His Body and Blood.

The Eight Principle Evil Thoughts

Jesus teaches us to be "wise as serpents" while we walk through this world. We must be sharp,

Pathways to Union with Jesus

sober-minded, and vigilant in guarding against the attacks of Satan our Enemy, who "prowls around like a roaring lion, seeking someone to devour." (1Peter 5:8)

"Look carefully then how you walk, not as unwise but as wise...(Eph 5:15 ff). "For we do not wrestle against flesh and blood, but against the rulers, against the authorities, against the cosmic powers over this present darkness". (Rm 6:12) "... so that we would not be outwitted by Satan; for we are not ignorant of his designs." (2Cor 2:11)

It is spiritual wisdom to understand who our Enemy is and his ways of leading us into sin. We have writings from early Christian ascetics of the late third century and forth centuries. These monks of the Desert in Egypt wisely examined their experience of temptation and tried to discover the patterns of the assaults of the demons.

Evagrius, (+399) writing in Greek, catalogued eight principal areas of temptation which he called "evil thoughts": gluttony, lust, greed, pride, envy, anger, vainglory, and discouragement. The last named is "acedia" in Greek. Acedia describes the ennui that settled upon ascetic monks in their protracted solitude. We would call it spiritual dryness or just plain boredom. The Latin Pope Gregory, (+602) later revised the list to give us the traditional Seven Deadly Sins.

The main pastoral purpose for calling our attention to these chief categories of temptation was to help us become spiritually vigilant and not surrender our free will to them.

Spiritual Warfare

An "evil thought" is any thought, feeling, memory, attraction, repulsion, or any psychological experience that inclines a person to think or act contrary to the truth and love of God as revealed to us in Jesus Christ. All evil thoughts come from the Evil One who intends to separate us from God and from our true identity by inviting us to sin. The evil spirits do not control or force us. They simply suggest an idea, word, feeling, or deed that is contrary to the truth and love of God revealed to us by Christ. Evil thoughts are always demonic lies disguised as truth.

We have the Holy Spirit within us. The indwelling Spirit gives us the power of discernment by which we can recognize the demonic deceit. Once an evil thought appears in our consciousness, we have a choice to make: either to submit ourselves to the lie or to contradict the lie with the truth God has revealed to us in Jesus. In our struggle to discern and reject evil thoughts sown in our hearts we are actually engaged in hand-to-hand combat with the demons of hell. In this battle, we rely totally of the power of Jesus in us, putting no confidence at all in the independent power of our own wisdom and strength. Christ defeats the Evil One for us, in us.

A Deeper Analysis Of Evil Thoughts

For many decades, and to my great advantage, I pursued purity of heart under the guidance of the ancient categories of the principle evil thoughts. However, eventually and reluctantly, I was forced by my experience to recognize that there are deeper and far more destructive evil thoughts than those listed by Evagrius and Pope Gregory. The categories of evil thoughts they identified are limited to temptations presented to the will. Experience of life has clearly shown me that moral actions express one's understanding of oneself and of God. If we have false notions of God and of ourselves our actions will likewise be wrong. How can we come to know, in truth, who we are and who God is? Thanks be to God, it is through Jesus Christ our Lord!

The Worst Evil Thoughts: False Ideas Of God And Of Self.

The erroneous ideas we have about God make it impossible to relate to God in truth and love. Until Christ enlightens us, we live with numerous erroneous notions about the character of God. These evil thoughts separate us from God. We may think of God as angry with us or as indifferent to us. Perhaps we see God as the Divine Judge… the Almighty Power… the aloof Eternal Intelligence, etc. Partial truths like these are totally inadequate to represent the heart of God. As we grow in faith under the teaching of the Spirit of Jesus, we gradually understand more deeply and clearly that God is infinitely compassionate, a tenderly caring Father and Mother…that God is our Self-sacrificing Friend Who takes delight in us, One Who loves us with pure grace-love. We relate to God rightly as we increasingly think rightly of God. Jesus, Who is the Radiance of the Father's Glory, causes us to know God and think rightly about God.

People do not behave directly from the reality of who they are. People behave from their consciousness of who they think they are. We relate to ourselves and to others according to the way we think of ourselves. Mistaken self-understanding makes

Pathways to Union with Jesus

it impossible to have true love for ourselves, for other people, and for God. Uninformed, misled, and deceived by our own fallen nature, by the judgments of the fallen world, and by the condemning lies of Satan, we are imprisoned by impressions and opinions about ourselves that have nothing to do with the truth of who we are in the mind of our Creator. We are what God makes us be.

Jesus is the Light of Revelation. The more we dwell with Him by meditating on scripture, by the prayer of loving attention to Him in our hearts, and by devoutly communing with Him in His Supper, the more we will personally realize that…

> "I am the eternally chosen of God. I am the everlasting desire of God. I am the joy of Jesus' heart. God loves me with all of His love. I am a unique created expression of the very Being of God. No one else in all creation manifests God and His Christ, Jesus, in the same way that I do. I am irreplaceable. God does not have another of me. I am His only one. God Alone is the infinite and eternal Unique One and it has pleased God to make me in His own image, a finite temporal unique one.

"Angels and saints who God allows to see my graced personal spirit fall into ecstasy. I am God's gift to all creation and I delight in giving myself to be enjoyed by all. Whoever knows me loves me. Whoever knows and loves me receives a particular fulfillment in beatitude that no one else can give. I am a lamp lit by the Light and it is my consummate joy to give my light to all in the house of God.

"My Father is Perfect and I am destined to become perfect. God, in the Spirit of Jesus, is even now making me perfect in thought and action. At present I am not yet perfect. I do not love God with *all* of my heart, soul, mind, body, and strength. I do not yet love myself perfectly. And therefore, I do not love all other people as I should love myself. I am a sinner. But I am a sinner whose sins are taken away. I am morally imperfect, but I am clothed and filled by grace with the perfection of Jesus Christ the Son of God.

Pathways to Union with Jesus

The Holy Spirit has revealed that God does not regard my sins at all. He does not judge me on account of them. Rather, God loves me totally on account of His Beloved Son Who gave Himself for me. Rightly, in my own eyes, I am imperfect. In God's eyes, rightly, I am perfect with the perfection of Jesus. I am holy with the holiness of Jesus. There is no rightful place at all in my life, in my thoughts, or in my feelings for any guilt and shame. These have been nailed to the cross and I am free of them. He carried them and I am completely free from their burden. Blessed be Jesus!

"Because God loves me totally and without regard to my sins, I want to love myself, sinner though I am, totally and without regard to my sins. Now I want to love all others, regardless of their sins, with the same grace-love with which God loves me.

"Every other person in all of God's creation has the same value and goodness and grace-love that I have. Every human being is my equal. In order to be complete in myself, I need and I want the gift that every single one of them is to me. Each one is a unique created expression of the Being of God. Each one of them (every human being) bestows upon me an incomparable beatific revelation of the goodness, beauty, truth, and grace-love of God. I esteem every person more than myself because each one is an image of God that I am not and I am eternally grateful to every one of them for being God's unique gift to me.

May we all become more and more truly conscious of God, of ourselves, and of others in this Light of Christ.

Purity Of Heart In Friendship With Jesus

I must include in this essay a new and wonderful understanding of purity of heart that God granted me while I was meditating on the passion of our Lord Jesus. Precisely, I was following the conversation Jesus had with His disciples at the Last Supper as recorded by John. In Chapter 13, we have the narrative of Jesus washing of the apostles' feet. The

Pathways to Union with Jesus

Greek word, "katharos", that is translated as "pure" in Mt 5:8 (Blessed are the pure in heart) is usually translated as "clean" in Jn 13:10. "Not all of you are clean." Our Lord was referring to the heart of Judas and not to the physical uncleanness of his feet. If we think about the difference between Judas and the other eleven, we will discover a new depth of the meaning of purity of heart.

If we ask what it is that makes the eleven pure (katharos) and Judas not pure, we will identify the worst of all evil thoughts: *Insincerity in friendship with Jesus.*

The eleven were morally very flawed and weak. They were not appreciably better than Judas in moral virtue. Their words and actions did not evince an enlightened consciousness about God and about themselves superior to that of Judas. For what reason, then, could our Lord call them "pure" or "clean" (katharos) and identify Judas as not "clean", not "pure in heart"? Answer: *The eleven were sincere in their relationship with Jesus*. In Gethsemane they would show themselves to be selfish, cowardly, ignorant, undependable, and even unfaithful. But they were also honest, without hypocrisy, sincere, "pure", in their very imperfect friendship with Jesus. Judas was a hypocrite, a lying pretender, faking his friendship with the Lord. Even his last expression of affection for Jesus was a hypocritical kiss of betrayal in Gethsemane.

We should have known from the beginning that purity of heart has to be a matter of our personal relationship of love for Jesus. God's final goal in the history of salvation is not to enforce right moral conduct, although morality has its own indispensible importance. Nor is God's saving work complete when He illumines our consciousness to know the truth about Him and about ourselves, although this revealed wisdom is of supreme value. From all eternity, through all of time, into all eternity to come, God wants only this: to have an interpersonal relationship of *sincere* love with each one of us.

The word 'sincere' comes from a Latin phrase, "sine cera" meaning "without wax". In ancient Rome, household items and images made of wood, clay, and metal were sold in the markets. Whenever an item had a flaw, scratch, hole or crack, the seller would fill the cavity with wax to make to appear unblemished. Items without flaws were sold at a higher price as "sine cera", without wax.

What Jesus wants from each of us is a simple, honest, direct relationship, just as we are, with all of our flaws and blemishes uncovered. No wax. A sincere friendship.

Friendship with Jesus brings us to the Father in this manner: God the Father brings all willing human beings into sincere friendship love with Jesus. Jesus, the Son of God, breathes His own Life-giving Spirit of Love into His friends. His Spirit in us makes us one with Jesus, the Beloved Son of God, eternally proceeding and returning to the Father in the Spirit of Filial Love.

A Pure Heart: A Sincere Relationship With Jesus

It is a great comfort and encouragement to us that our Blessed Lord Jesus called the Eleven who sat with Him at the Supper, "pure". If they were ignorant and morally flawed, yet they were pure in heart, so we, though no less ignorant and morally flawed, have hope to called pure in heart by Jesus.

To be "pure in heart" all we sinners need to do is trust in Jesus completely. We do not need to be morally better than we are; we just need to be with Him in our true humble condition just as we are, without any pretense, hiding, or self-exalting illusion. This is an outrageous paradox: Only those who know they are infected with selfishness, lacking in love, and grossly ignorant of the ways and will of God can relate to Jesus sincerely and without hypocrisy.

This humble sincerity has nothing in common with self-condemnation. Sincere Christians are not wickedly depraved. Not at all! Groveling in self-denigration has no place in Christian life. Christian humility comes from awareness of falling short of the divine perfection to which we are called: "You, therefore, must be perfect as your heavenly Father is perfect". (Mt 5:48) If we misunderstand this sentence of our Lord to be only a commandment, we are hopeless. But it is not just a new and impossible requirement. The commandments of Jesus are prophecies and promises: they produce what they demand of those who trust in Him.

Our perfection is not a product of our moral behavior. The divine perfection to which we are called is the gift of God. During our life in this world, we are called and empowered by the Spirit to moral improvement. Our moral improvement in this world is a seed and a sign of the total perfection that shall be ours when we join Jesus in the Father's house.

During the time of our humiliation in this mortal life, we fix our eyes on Jesus, Jesus Who loves us to the point of taking our guilt, our condemnation, and our death upon Himself. To behold Him loving us with so great a love and at the same time knowing how broken and unworthy we are, is to be honest, sincere, and pure in heart. The revelation of His love instills confident hope in those of pure heart that we shall see Him Face to Face and become like Him in His Glory.

A Pure Heart: A Grateful Heart

A Christian of pure heart engages in personal relationship with God by gazing in faith upon the face of Jesus Who dwells in our hearts. In our exchange of personal mutual loving awareness with Jesus, we present ourselves as we are, having nothing of our own to give and burdened with our moral weakness and mental ignorance. But also, we present ourselves to Christ in contemplative prayer with an insatiable hunger for God. We are sincere and therefore pure when we relate to Him in the truth of our poverty, need, and spiritual hunger. This emptiness allows God to illumine our consciousness with the revelation of the grace-love that we have in Christ. God makes us know we are beloved, beloved independently of our sins, weaknesses, and ignorance, beloved with God's love of delight in us! When God's

Pathways to Union with Jesus

incomprehensibly great love for us shines upon us, we feel gratitude beyond description.

First God reveals the Gift. We receive His revelation by faith. Then we experience the Gift. Experience produces joyful awareness and grateful acknowledgement of the Gift and of the Giver: Jesus is the Gift given by the Father. The Gift of God is ever present to us in time and in eternity, undiminished, unwavering, permanent, constant, unconditionally bestowed and never retracted. Gratitude is our very first response when we become aware of the Gift of God. Gratitude draws us to give ourselves wholly to the One Who gives Himself wholly to us. The measure of our gratitude is the measure of our purity of heart.

"Blessed Are The Pure In Heart For They Shall See God."

Jesus of Nazareth

TO THE PATHWAY OF LECTIO DIVINA

At baptism, or upon our adult conversion, we turned away from our old pathways of life in the flesh, with its deceitful and degrading worldly goals. We began to run a new course of life in the Spirit.

Pathways to Union with Jesus

We know the destination of our spiritual journey: Purity of Heart in this life giving way to Glory in the Life to come.

Now we begin to chart our course through the Pathways. Although we travel the pathways to Jesus simultaneously in our lives, we separate them in writing for the purpose of individual study.

The first pathway that we will consider is the most fundamental: Lectio Divina. It includes many forms of communication with God, the Principal Author of Holy Scripture. The Father came to us in the Word Incarnate. We return to the Father in the same Word whom we encounter in the inspired words of Holy Scripture.

We proceed now to the study of Lectio Divina.

CHAPTER TWO

THE PATHWAY OF LECTIO DIVINA

LECTIO DIVINA

The Spiritual Way Of The Word

Jesus is the Word of God. Through Him and in Him all things are made. For God spoke and all creation came to be. Jesus has within Himself all of the words of God in creation and in Scripture. Inspired by God, the human words of the bible are sacraments of The Divine Word: Jesus. God is the Principal author of the Holy Scriptures. Therefore, even the most prosaic and least revelatory words of Scripture have a special holiness and richness beyond their literal human meaning.

The Latin expression, "Lectio Divina" (pronounced: "lex'-ee-oh di-veen'-ah") can be translated as "divine reading", "reading divine things", or "sacred reading". The meaning, however, is much deeper and broader than these translations suggest. As a summary description, we can say: *Lectio Divina is a personal engagement with the Holy Spirit while prayerfully reading scripture that engenders unlimited experiences of spiritual healing and growth, illumination of mind and heart, transformation of consciousness, and contemplation of God and the mysteries of God.*

The Real Presence of Jesus in Scripture

Recognizing the real presence of Christ is of the greatest importance for those who practice lectio divina. This is a deep mystery and must be expressed carefully in order not to err or confuse. I do not say the physical book of the scriptures bears the Real Presence of Jesus. I believe, and I now ask you to discern and believe, that *when a Christian reads the Holy Scriptures with faith and love, Jesus is really present to the believer and His Presence is as Real as His Presence to His disciples when He appeared to them after His resurrection.*

The real presence of Jesus in lectio divina is not physical and external; it is spiritual and interior to the heart. This is one of the ways He fulfills His promise to come to us and manifest Himself to us. (cf. Jn 14:21-23)

How Jesus is Present in Lectio Divina

Jesus is present to the believer in lectio divina as the Light of Revelation. Let me explain this assertion.

The human words written on the pages of the Bible do not, of themselves and by themselves, reveal God and the mysteries of God. If they did, everyone who reads the Scriptures would become believers. Some atheists read the Bible and remain atheists. Members of other religions read the Bible and do not abandon their religion in favor of Christianity. Many secular humanists and non-Christian students of comparative religion also read the Bible, without finding themselves recipients of divine revelation. No, the printed pages of Scripture do not by themselves have the power to make God's revelation known.

Jesus is the Light of revelation. He shines within the heart enabling the Bible reader to know God's revelation in the words of Scripture. From the moment a person hears or reads the word of God *and recognizes it as the revelation of God*, Jesus the Revealer is present as Divine Light. Without the Presence of the Inner Light of Jesus, the Scriptures we read would merely be the words of men expressing their religious thoughts. Our experience of knowing God and God's mysteries when we practice lectio divina gives us personal conviction of the Real Presence of Jesus, The Light of Revelation.

The Personal Meaning Of Scripture

To believers, only the Christian Scriptures give infallible witness to the final objective public and

Pathways to Union with Jesus

revelation of God given to the whole world for the salvation of all. Christian interpretation of Scripture is personal and fallible. Therefore, no one should expect other people to believe or obey his or her own subjective personal understanding of scripture! Nevertheless, God does speak subjectively and personally to each believer who draws near to Him in a self-surrendering reading of Scripture. These meanings are personal. They are loving communications between God and the person He is feeding with His word. The Father instructs each child individually by means of the Scriptures personally understood. An example from the life of St. Anthony of the Desert will make this point clear.

This event took place about the year 270 in a Christian Church in Alexandria in Egypt. The twenty-year-old Anthony heard the Gospel read at the Sunday celebration of the Holy Eucharist. The gospel passage was taken from Mark, chapter ten. The text recounts the meeting between our Blessed Lord and the rich young man who had kept the commandments from his youth. "And Jesus looking upon him loved him, and said to him, 'You lack one thing; go, sell all that you have, and give to the poor, and you will have treasure in heaven, and come follow me.'" (Mk 10: 21) O*bjectively,* these words had not been addressed to Anthony. S*ubjectively,*

Pathways to Union with Jesus

God directed them to Anthony. Anthony received them as God's personal word to him. He left the church, sold all he had, gave the proceeds to the poor, and went out to follow Jesus spiritually in the desert for the rest of his long life. God raised up Anthony to become the first person in history who was not a martyr and yet was recognized as a saint in the church. His example and teaching still inspire Christians so many centuries later. All this happened because he was receptive to God's personal communication to him through the words of Scripture.

Fellow Christians, we must become familiar with this idea and be ready to receive the gift frequently. God will speak to you, personally and individually, as you submit yourself to Him in your lectio divina. People who read the Bible only as a record of God's word to other people or to all people in general, have not yet practiced lectio divina. Lectio divina is a personal conversation between God and the reader. God will show you the objective meanings of Scripture that He intends all people to understand. And God will also give meanings to the words of Scripture that are for you alone.

Preparing For Lectio Divina: Spiritual Hunger

The pre-condition for lectio divina, and the attitude which distinguishes it from simply "reading the bible," is that one who engages in lectio divina must have a deep desire for transforming union with Jesus by means of the scriptural word. It will do us little good to read the Scriptures unless we have *a passionate hunger for the fullness of Life in the Spirit.* God does not, and cannot, give us gifts that we do not value and desire. If we only knew the Gift of God, we would ask with all the ardor of our soul, and He would give us the Water of eternal life to drink! So let us thirst, ask, and drink from the well of divine grace in lectio divina.

The Proper Dispositions For The Practice Of Lectio Divina

Reverent Fear

First, we must be *seeking God with reverent fear.* We go to scripture as to the place where we will meet the God. The prospect of meeting the Holy God should arouse in us a holy fear. It is impossible to meet with God and not be drastically changed. In regard to our fleshly selfishness, it is impossible to meet God without dying. God is a Vine Dresser. We are the vine branches. The Word of God is the pruning knife. Much has to be cut away, so that we may bear more fruit. It hurts, but it makes us grow and bear more fruit. In your lectio divina you must expect to be put to death in the flesh and raised up to new life in the Spirit!

Our holy fear of God should extend to a *great reverence for the book of Scriptures* that contains His Word. We should handle the physical book of the scriptures with a tenderness, reverence, and respect that we do not give to any other book. We have a natural reverence for symbols of mere human beings whom we love. None of us would use a photograph of a beloved mother or spouse as a blotter or scratch pad. How much more ought we to revere the book of God's testimony of His love for us! Always honor the Book. Keep it in a place of honor. Do not put things on top of it. It is more valuable to you than anything else written in the whole world. Show your love and reverence by the way you touch this blessed book from God. Do not even look at your Bible carelessly, but when you see it think of God and of His love for you expressed in the Book.

Surrender

We must be ready to surrender to God and to His judgment that will confront us in Scripture. Scripture has the power to slay us and it has power to raise us up, *if* we surrender ourselves to its power to kill and to make alive again. We can, as many do while reading Scripture, hide from this sword of the Spirit. Scripture must first slay us in our pride and complacency in order to raise us up as humble and devout women and men of God. Refusal to be slain by the sword of God's word is the chief reason why people are not being raised to new life by the Scriptures. Surrender to the sword of the Word. Surrender also to the resurrection power of the Word.

Submission

In regard to all other books, we ought to read critically. We should weigh, measure, and pass judgment upon what we read. With regard to Sacred Scripture, our attitude must be the reverse. *We submit ourselves to Scripture to be measured, weighed, and judged by it.* Scripture will lift us to the understanding of divine things. At the same time, it will also bring us low by revealing to us how far we are from the true knowledge and complete love of God. The written revelation will make us shudder when it shows us how much we have to suffer for the sake of the Name of Jesus. If we submit to the authority of Scripture it will give us courage to face all these hard things, because the same Word reveals to us the divine power we have from the Spirit Who dwells in us.

Practicing Lectio Divina

The earth is a sphere with innumerable points on its surface. We speak in general of directions as being north, east, south and west. The four points of the compass refer to general directions, each of which includes countless places. Similarly, we group the countless experiences of Sacred Reading of the Scriptures in four general categories as: Reading, Meditation, Prayer, and Contemplation. These four words translate the Medieval Latin: Lectio, Meditatio, Oratio, Contemplatio. We will reflect on these four "directions" in which the Spirit carries us when we practice Sacred Reading.

I READING

Lectio, *reading, is the simple act of reading the Scriptures as one who is seeking God, seeking His truth for your life, seeking His salvation, seeking all He has to give you and all He has to ask of you.*

Scripture first. It is possible to use other spiritual writings about union with God in Christ as subject matter for lectio divina. However, we should not fill our reading time with other spiritual books (including this one!) unless we consistently spend significant amounts of time using the Scriptures, especially the New Testament, for lectio divina. I strongly urge anyone who has not fulfilled that prerequisite to set other spiritual books aside for a time and concentrate on the Scriptures. If you have made a good beginning with the Scriptures, there is no reason why you cannot read other books. Only do not let other reading take the place of, or curtail, your lectio divina of Scripture.

Place to Start

Beginners should first dedicate themselves to lectio divina in the New Testament. The New Testament is the key to understanding what was written in the Old Testament. In the New Testament, give priority and emphasis to the four Gospels, because these books are primarily concerned with presenting Jesus, the Divine Word made flesh and the Savior of the world. To one well versed in the whole New Testament, the Old will yield its deepest meaning. In the Old Testament, the Psalms offer the best initial material for lectio. Next, the Wisdom books and the Prophets lend themselves more readily to lectio divina. We need some preliminary historical commentary on the prophets in order to understand their message. Read commentaries outside the time you set apart for lectio divina lest you replace spiritual lectio divina with intellectual biblical study. The historical books of the Old Testament are studded with precious antetypes and foreshadows of Christ and the New Covenant, but you will also read of numerous revolting events, actions, and thoughts in the Old Testament Bible that are totally irreconcilable with the Kingdom of God that Jesus brought to earth.

Duration and Frequency

The *duration* of lectio should be twenty to thirty minutes minimum. Still, ten or fifteen minutes would be a whole world better than nothing! Occasionally, perhaps on a Sunday, holiday, or retreat day, you might spend hours fruitfully engaged in lectio. It can really be a wonderful spiritual refreshment. *Frequency* should be as close to daily as possible, with an absolute minimum of three times a week. There is no obligation concerning time given to lectio divina, but a trustworthy counsel for beginners is: "more is better". Nevertheless, the length of time spent in lectio should not be extended so far as to impede the fulfillment of ones other duties of Christian life.

When

Lectio, for most people, can best be practiced in the early morning, before the start of the workday. This presumes you get to bed in time to give yourself your needed rest. A person who is not rested is not physically fit to practice lectio or the Jesus Prayer. You can certainly dedicate your sleep as a prayer but you cannot practice lectio divina while you sleep. Get rested first, then pray or practice lectio.

If a person is energetic and alert, there is no reason why lectio (or the Jesus Prayer) cannot be done in the evening before bed. Some people put their time of lectio divina immediately before or after the time they set apart for the Jesus Prayer. Lectio can prepare for and spontaneously lead into the Jesus Prayer. A few people find it helpful to get up by alarm clock during the middle of the night to dedicate a quiet time to lectio or to the Jesus Prayer. Using the "middle of the night" for these devotions is in direct line with the ancient religious practice of vigils.

Where

We are in the body in space. Physical surroundings always influence our mind and heart. The tradition has proven effective that we should dedicate a special place *exclusively* for our lectio and our prayer. You will find it helpful to consecrate a prayer room or a small empty closet. If that is impossible, at least select a piece of furniture as your 'prayer chair'. One man I know habitually uses a special chair facing the wall adorned with a cross. The place you choose becomes holy. Soon, that sacred place will call out to you to enter God's Presence in prayer and lectio.

How

First, make a preparatory prayer in this manner. Kneel down and fold your hands devoutly. If that is physically too challenging, just kneel before God in your heart. Then remember how unworthy you are to receive God's Self-revelation. Remember how great, high, and holy God's revelation is. Next, ask for three things: 1) Ask God to cleans your heart by His grace and mercy so that you may be a vessel worthy to receive His Holy Word. If you have any unconfused sins tell them humbly to God now and be forgiven. (2) Ask God to give you the Spirit to enlighten your mind to understand His Word. (3) Finally, ask God to give you grace and strength to carry out the truth of His Will that you are about to read in Scripture.

Stay kneeling (if only in heart). Begin reading the sacred text on your knees for a verse or two. This is a devotional act of religious reverence by which you honor God's holy word. Then rise, take your seat comfortably, and continue your reading.

Always Read Meaningfully and Slowly

Do not read in a hurry. Try to pronounce each word (mentally if not physically) in the tone in which it seems to have been meant originally. At lectio, we read and hear the words " Come, follow me." in a tone and sentiment far different than, " Crucify him!"

Never try to finish a certain quantity of text within a certain time limit. Read each word, passage, and page as if it were all there were to read in Scripture. Our forbears in the faith believed that any one page, even a single sentence, from the Holy Bible contains enough wisdom and grace to guide and sanctify our whole lives. Quantity of text is not a value. The depth and completeness of our appropriation of the text is what matters. Suppose, for instance, that anyone fully believed, fully experienced, and lived by this one sentence of our beloved Lord Jesus: "I am the vine; you are the branches." (Jn 15: 5) That person would not need any other Scripture or anything else but would become perfect in holiness. Please be convinced: The quality of one's absorption, not the quantity of text, transforms the one who reads Scripture. In the sections below on Meditation and Prayer, we will see how to better absorb the word of God.

Open Minded Reading

In your reading, do not cling to pre-conceived notions. Do not read previously understood meanings into a fresh reading of a biblical text. Allow the Lord to reveal new things to you. Read with a desire and readiness to receive the "Fullness of Life" in whatever way Jesus wants to give it to you, *this time*. As Scripture texts reveal new things to you, be ready to renounce any wrong ideas you may have had about God, yourself, other people, and the world. The text remains the same when we re-read a passage of Scripture, but God continually opens up new and deeper meanings.

Recognize Jesus

You will joyfully recognize Jesus present in everything that is true, good, noble, beautiful, loving, and hopeful in what you read in Scripture. In any part of the Old Testament or the New, when truth, light, love, righteousness, goodness, joy, hope, life, mercy, forgiveness, etc are demonstrated, mentioned, or only implied, you will recognize the presence of our Beloved Lord Jesus. Similarly, you will painfully feel the absence of Jesus in everything untrue, evil, cruel, deceitful, violent, unloving, or despairing in what you read in the Bible. All that is good reveals Jesus' presence. All that is evil reveals Jesus' absence. Thus, for instance, I can see only the absence of Jesus in the cruel slaughter of all of the inhabitants of Ai recounted in Joshua 8. But the account in Genesis 33: 4 -10 of the forgiveness Esau gave to Jacob is a beautiful prefiguration of the forgiving love of Jesus.

Identification

At conception, any human being has the possibility of growing up in millions of different ways. Any one of us "formed" adults could have been formed in countless other ways. At birth, our personality is amorphous and plastic. In the course time, under the influences of our unique experiences, each personality is formed in his or her own way. All of the other ways of being human that we see in other people are possibilities that were not actualized in us. With that in mind, let us consider the people we meet in Scripture.

No person in the Bible is so bad that you cannot admit and repent of the same evil in yourself, at least to some degree and by way of possibility. We have either committed the offense, or without the preventive grace of God, we could have committed the offenses of others recorded in Scripture. Likewise, no one in the Bible is so blessed by God that we do not share in his or her blessing.

Each of us must read God's election of Moses at the burning bush as his or her own divine election. Moses' privileged knowledge of God was only a foreshadow of ours. We can and we should identify ourselves with all of the friends and saints of God. The biblical histories of all those elect of old were written to reveal to us who we are in Jesus. Dare to believe and say: "The lives of Elijah, Samuel, David and all the kings, priests, and prophets of the Old Testament dimly foreshadow my life in Jesus". As you read of them, feel their feelings, pray their prayers, do their good deeds, own their guilt, make your own their holy aspirations, their sufferings, and their grace.

Pathways to Union with Jesus

This is the truth about you in Jesus Christ. But we must also acknowledge that the deceitfulness of Jacob, the murmuring of the Israelites, the lust of David, the cruelty of Absalom, the denials of Peter, and, yes, even the betrayal of Judas—all of these evils, too, are potentially in us. That acknowledgement inspires us to ask for grace as it opens our minds to how much we need Jesus to be Our Savior!

Beyond gaining your intellectual assent, I am urging upon you the *devotional practice of identification*. In this devotion, you use your imagination, your emotions, and your will. You put yourself in the circumstances of the biblical personages. You feel what they feel. You say their words as your words, or hear what they heard, as if spoken to you. There is in you a prophet Nathan and in his spirit, you speak truth to power confronting the sinful king David: "You are the man!" But you are also the accused adulterous murderer and you bow your head in shame, sorrow, and repentance, as you hear the same words hurled at you. Then, with the penitent heart of David you confess, "I have sinned against the Lord!" Shout out loud your wishful loyalty to Jesus in Peter's words: "If I must die with you I will not deny you!" Then feel the eyes of Jesus as he looks into your eyes from across the courtyard of Caiaphas…and go out and weep bitterly with the tears of the denying coward

Peter. You are Bartimaeus the blind beggar. Cry out, "Jesus, son of David, have mercy on me!" Do not let any bystander stop you from crying out. Shout all the louder: "Jesus, son of David, have mercy on me!" Realize that you are the leper who falls at Jesus feet saying, "Lord, if you will, you can make me clean". Hear the loving words of the Savior spoken to you, "I will. Be clean!" Feel the joy! This scripture is about you, here and now.

Seek the Heart of Jesus

In antiquity, Jewish culture and language did not have the clear distinct mental categories for emotion, thought, and volition that we have developed in the last few hundred years. Our categorical distinctions have value but at the same time they ignore the relative mutual inclusion of feeling, thinking, and willing. The New Testament authors do not focus on feelings; they focus on actions. Actions are the final effects that express the sum total of one's mind, heart, and will.

Human emotions played their part in the actions of Jesus. Seeking the heart of Jesus means recognizing the emotions of Jesus and, at least by desire and prayer, making His emotions our own. As we know by painful experience, we do not have voluntary control over the way we feel. That lack of power, however, does not prevent us from appreciating, desiring, and asking God for the beautiful and holy emotions of Jesus we see revealed in the New Testament.

Our Lord's feelings are generally not mentioned in the Gospel narratives of the events that He experienced. How did Jesus feel about Himself and about the Baptist, when He heard John publicly declare of Him, "Behold the Lamb of God!"? What were the Lord's feelings when He took the little children in his arms and blessed them? What sentiments arose in the heart of Christ when His beloved friend Judas betrayed Him in the Garden with a kiss?

With the humble tentativeness, with prayer, and with trust in the illumination of the Holy Spirit, we may imagine the unstated emotions of our Blessed Lord. Even the emotions of the incarnate Son of God are divine revelations, worthy of uttermost religious reverence.

On occasion, the feelings of Jesus are directly noted in the Gospels. We ought to take them deeply into our consideration and our prayer. For example, see His heart of gratitude as He gave solemn thanks and praise to His Father when He saw while the

Pathways to Union with Jesus

wise, learned, and powerful of the land did not receive Him, the little ones, the ordinary people, even the outcast sinners were drawn to Him. (Mt 11: 25-26) Feel His sorrow as He wept over the blindness and the suffering of His beloved Jerusalem. (Lk 19: 41-42) Sense His frustration, sorrow, and anger as He looked around in the synagogue at worshippers who were plotting to kill Him if He would heal the man with the withered hand on the Sabbath. (MK 3: 1-6)

The strongest waves of emotion that swept through he heart of Jesus were feelings of immeasurably great adoring love toward the Father and infinite compassion toward sinners in their suffering. Imagine His holy emotions while he spent whole nights in "the prayer of God". (The quotation is the literal translation of the Greek of Luke 6:12)! Consider the reverent love and trust in His heart as He offered 'The Lord's Prayer' to the Father on our behalf. (Mt 6: 9:13) Think of the indescribable emotions of adoration, desire, and love Jesus expressed in His prayer to the Father at the Last Supper. (Jn 17)

Appreciate His feelings for His friends: "Jesus loved Martha and her sister Mary and Lazarus". Imagine the ocean of compassion He felt when He saw the sorrowful widow of Nain as she walked behind the bier of her dead son. What rush of emotions did He feel at the Last Supper when, "having loved his own who were in the world, he loved them to the end"? (Jn 13:1). Contemplate Jesus "very sorrowful, even to death" when He took our sorrows upon Himself. (Mt 26:38)

Dear Ones, prayerful adoring contemplation of the holy emotions of Jesus as seen in the Gospels transforms our hearts into the heart of Jesus. Amen.

Reading in the Eternal Present

Eternity is misunderstood when it is thought of as "time without beginning or end". Eternity is God possessing in Himself all of the creatures that proceed from Him all at once. He possesses all things, simultaneously, in the indivisible instant of His Eternal Being. Time began when God breathed forth the first creature. Time will end when the last creature attains to the glory for which it was eternally predestined by the Father in the Son through the Holy Spirit. The end of time will arrive when the Lord Jesus returns to take all those who belong to Him into His eternal glory in resurrected spiritual bodies.

Beings that begin to exist and cease to exist are temporal. They exist only for a while. Temporal beings come out of their eternal Creator. As long as it exists, every temporal being and Eternal God exist together, the way a song exists together simultaneously with the singer.

Temporal *beings* exist in extra-mental reality. Time exists only as a thought, a being of the mind. Time is a mental instrument of measurement, like numbers. We imagine an endless time-line in our mind. Then we record on that imaginary time-line the succession of our physical and psychological experiences in relation to each other as "before or after" in arbitrary units we call seconds, minutes… millennia.

Temporal beings of the past and of the future do not now exist in time. However, they have a permanent presence to God in His Eternity. All that will be and happen in the future of our temporal world has an eternal pre-existence in the eternity of God. All that once was but no longer exists in time has a post-existence in the eternity of God. These creatures come to be and cease to be in the temporal world, but they always exist within the Eternal Being of God.

The New Testament contains many statements that make sense only by understanding the

Pathways to Union with Jesus

simultaneous inclusion of all things past and future in God's Eternal Present. Consider the following. Jesus declared that the long dead patriarchs are alive to God because "all live to him". (Lk 20:38)

The Pharisees, who could not think of anything outside the framework of time, objected to our Lord's saying that Abraham had seen Him. "Your father Abraham rejoiced that he would see my day. He saw it and was glad. So the Jews said to him, 'You are not yet fifty years old and you have seen Abraham?' Jesus said to them, 'Truly, truly, I say to you, before Abraham was, I am.'" (Jn 8:56-58)

St. Paul alluded to this Christian understanding of the "contemporaneity' of eternity with all time past and future when He wrote: "And those whom he pre-destined [past] he also called, and those whom he called he also justified [present] and those whom he justified he also glorified [future]." (Rm 8:30) Here Paul speaks of our historically past predestination, our present condition as justified, and our future glorification with Jesus as events that are present reality. This makes perfect sense when understood by faith as referring to the "eternal present" of God.

Jesus died and rose from the dead in the historical past. Our physical resurrection is in the future.

Paul puts them together in God's eternal present, saying: God has "raised us up" with Jesus in Eph 2:6. In the book of Revelation, chapter 21, John describes the New Jerusalem coming down out of heaven from God —surely an event to come in the future at the return of the Lord, but already present in God's eternity where John sees it in his vision.

By faith we have been born again into eternal life in our personal spirit. In our eternal personal spirit we are passing through this temporal life. Our personal eternal life is hid with Christ in God, while we carry out our mission in time to the people to whom we are sent. Our eternal personal spirit (πνευμα = pneuma) is present in this world through our mortal body (σομα = soma) that is made alive in this world by our temporal soul (ψυχη = psyche).

You are one with Jesus as He is one with the Father. In your personal spirit, brothers and sisters in Christ, you share the eternal life and mind of Christ. When nonbelievers read the biblical report of past or future things and events, they know nothing more than the human images and thoughts in their minds suggested by the text. But you, O Christian, when you read, or even just call to mind, the past and future things God has revealed to you, you know

Pathways to Union with Jesus

them as present reality in the Eternal Life of God that you share in Christ.

We are reflecting upon "awareness by faith" of God's past and future events. We do not have physical presence to these things. God does not give us any supernatural vision, sense impression, or imagination of the realities we know in God by faith. By God's revelation, we can have access to past and future things *only* as an experience of conscious awareness in our personal spirit. One who does not have the light of faith merely *imagines* the birth of Jesus in Bethlehem. One who believes God's revelation *knows* the birth of Christ.

To imagine something is one thing. To be present to it in conscious awareness is something for greater. In spirit, not in body, a person of faith reading Scripture can be present in awareness when God *is* creating the world… when God *is* delivering His people from Egyptian bondage… when Jesus *is* being born in Bethlehem… when He *is* teaching, healing, casting out demons… when He is dying on the cross, rising from the dead, and reigning gloriously in the New Jerusalem. Yes, these things remain past and future in the experience of our time-bound soul and body. But to our spirits, already raised into the Life of

God, they are eternally present because "all things live to God".

It is difficult to grasp how the Christian has access in his or her spirit to events past and future in the eternity of God. However, it is the same thing as prayer. Whenever a Christian prays she or he enters into the conscious presence of God the Father and Jesus in eternity. If it is marvelous that we have supernatural power to be consciously aware of God in Eternity, isn't it far less marvelous to be consciously aware of the past and future created realities that exist eternally in God?

When we read of past and future things of God in Scripture, we should be aware of them as realities now present to us in the timeless eternity of God. We can remember the scriptural details of the passion of Christ. Far more than that, by faith we can be present in awareness to these events, events that culminate in His death and resurrection for the salvation of human beings of all time.

Lectio Divina Forms The Mind Of Christ

The Spirit of grace gradually transforms the believer in the image of Christ. Our earthly mentality diminishes. The Mind of Christ increases within us. Increasingly we think, feel, understand, evaluate, and judge the world and our life experiences the way Jesus does. Lectio divina is the laboratory of the transformation of our minds. In the Scriptures, we seek and find the Mind of Jesus and it becomes our own mind.

The secular news media record the phantasms of unbelief that pass through the unredeemed collective consciousness. Empires, kingdoms, democracies, elections, wars, famines, crimes and plagues: they all come and go. They melt one into another, leaving no meaning and no salvation behind. But the Saving Word of the Lord endures forever. Christian faith interprets what happens in human history in the light of biblical revelation.

The Bible reveals all historical events as gathered into God's plan for human salvation. Scripture reveals the meaning in the Mind of Christ of the things that happen in our lives and in the whole world. Lectio divina enables us to know, at the deepest theological level, what is going on in our lives and in the world today. The sum total of human suffering in the world is immeasurable and unspeakably evil. The good news is that God is taking over; His Kingdom is coming –even using the evils we sinners bring into this world to accomplish His Will.

And His Will is Eternal Life for all who are willing to receive it.

Lectio divina reveals to us who we are. No picture or description of you can tell you about yourself as profoundly as the Bible does. Neither science, nor psychology, nor art, nor any other human source will enable you to know the deepest truth about yourself that Scripture reveals to you. We have a famous saying from the early Fathers of the Church: "Ignorance of the Scriptures is ignorance of Christ." Isn't that a great sentence! And here is another one, like it: "Ignorance of the Scriptures is ignorance of yourself." Scripture is the story of your life, written by your Author. Read it in faith and you will become it.

Each one of us was created to be conformed to the image of the Son of God. As our scriptural knowledge of Jesus grows, we see ever more clearly the kind of persons we are becoming. The nature of our personal spirit may be likened to a mirror. A mirror takes on the form of whatever is placed in front of it. In lectio divina, our spirit stands before the Word of God, Jesus. We see Him and become like Him. Knowing Jesus we know ourselves. "And we all, with unveiled face, beholding the glory of the Lord, are being changed into his likeness from one degree of glory to another…" (2Cor 3:18)

II MEDITATION

Meditatio. "Meditation" is a word with a wide variety of very diverse meanings. Happily, we can leave all but one of them out of consideration. The meaning of "meditation" in the tradition of biblical prayer we are following is very clear and simple: *Biblical meditation means repetition of a bible text by heart.*

As we read along in Scripture, the Holy Spirit is intensely active within our hearts. He is the Divine Physician who manages our spiritual health care. The Divine Spirit decides what we need most at any given point on our spiritual journey. Accordingly, to free us from some burden of sin or error, or to bestow a special revelation or gift upon us, He causes certain verses to arrest our attention and impress themselves upon us.

We may have read a particular verse dozens or hundreds of times before. But there may come a time when the Spirit chooses to use this verse in the present moment to correct an error, clear up a doubt, convict us of a hitherto unrecognized and unrepented sin, or to evoke in us a desire for some spiritual gift we have not yet recognized and desired from God.

For instance, perhaps you are unconsciously failing to trust God's loving providence for your life. You are feeling vaguely anxious. You do not consciously focus on the anxiety nor ask yourself why you are feeling it. In such a case, the Spirit might act upon you in the following way. You happen to be reading through the psalms. As you are reading along, perhaps in Ps 9, you "accidentally" hit on this verse (10):

> "...those who know Thy Name will put their trust in Thee;
> For Thou O Lord, hast not forsaken those who seek Thee"

Upon reading these words, your heart grows warm, you feel drawn to these pleasant words. They are illumining and healing your heart. The Spirit is drawing you to them. The words seem sweet and beautiful, powerfully true, and they attract you. It is given to you from above to know that these simple words contain all the wisdom and nourishment that you need now. The Spirit is healing your lack of trust and your anxiety

When our experience is like this, we should leave off our slow deliberate reading. Instead, we should re-read the words that God has "highlighted" in our hearts. We should read them repeatedly. Soon we will know them by heart. Then we might close our eyes and let our heart recite the same words over, perhaps to the rhythm of our heartbeat or breath. Again and again, as long as we are attracted to do so, we should "meditate" this word of God in our hearts in this fashion. Do not be led into discursive meditation, which means analysis and rumination of the text. Do that analysis and rumination at another time. Right now, you are entrusting yourself to the healing power of God's word. We are not entrusting ourselves to the power of our own best thoughts about God's word. Just repeat the same words of Scripture over and over in your heart. Listen to them, feel them, mean them, and yield yourself to them.

We can liken the words of God in Scripture to seed. By repeating the words we bury them in the soil of our hearts; we give them time to sink roots deep in our consciousness. God's word is like oil poured out in lamps to give light or poured out as a remedy. By meditation through repetition, we illumine our spiritual darkness and anoint the wounds of our soul with the light-giving and healing oil of the word.

After the time devoted to Lectio Divina, it is a good practice to write down in one place each text

God gives you to meditate. That growing list will be a spiritual treasury for you in the future. Another good practice, outside the time of lectio divina, is to write down the text you have meditated on a paper or card and stick it on your bathroom mirror. Or better, carry it around with you in your pocket. As God gives the inclination and opportunity, you can take out the card and repeat the text again from time to time during the day. You will find that "chains" of special scripture texts develop for you. Chains of Bible verses grow as you add each new meditated text to your collection and you will see how wonderfully they illuminate each other.

After you have meditated a text for a while, you will begin to feel that it is no longer desirable to continue repeating the words. The text itself will no longer have power to attract you. That is the time to resume your sacred reading. Just go back to the place where you left off and continue reading in your lectio divina.

We have to appreciate how great a spiritual gift is the simple act of reading scripture. Sisters and Brothers, no one ever takes up the Bible to read it in faith except by being moved by the Holy Spirit. The Father gives us the attraction to Jesus in the Scripture. Then, by power of the Holy Spirit, we carry out the holy desire in the blessed act of reading the Holy Scriptures. Once we have entered the Garden of the Lord, Sacred Scripture, the Holy Spirit keeps on doing wonderful new and surprising things to us for our healing, our growth, and our happiness.

Now that we have considered the spiritual gift of meditation that the Spirit gives to the biblical seeker of God, let us go on to reflect on another vast universe of graces that come to us in lectio divina: praying the Scriptures.

III PRAYER

Oratio. Prayer is a gift of the Holy Spirit bestowed during lectio divina. It is an inspired response to God about what He is saying to us in His word.

Biblically inspired prayer changes our lectio divina from a simple act of listening to God into a conversation with Him. As in any conversation, one person responds to what the other person is saying. In this case, the Other is God.

The impulse we feel to pray during our sacred reading arises from the personal meaning we find in the Scripture. The *objective meaning of Scripture is that which the human and divine authors originally intended to be conveyed by the inspired words.* The objective meaning is the literal meaning that scripture scholars and students seek to understand. However, when a Christian today reads the Scriptures, God speaks to that person in the present moment. *The personal meaning of Scripture is the particular meaning that God intends for each person at the moment of His visitation while they are reading His word.*

The 'objective meaning' of Scripture is more important for the sake of preaching of the Gospel, for biblical theology, and for a common understanding of Revelation among God's people down through the ages. The 'personal meaning' of scripture has special importance for the spiritual growth of the individual Christian. The 'personal meaning' is what God is saying to me, revealing to me, here and now. My prayer response to God flows from my subjective understanding of the text.

True And False Personal Meanings

How can we distinguish between a "pious illusion" and an authentic divinely intended personal meaning of Scripture? We use this criterion of discernment: No personal meaning can be from God if it conflicts with the objective meaning of any passage of

Pathways to Union with Jesus

Scripture. Examples will make this easier to understand. The story of St. Anthony, recalled above, exemplifies a true personal meaning of Scripture. His personal meaning was consistent with the objective meaning of the text and with the whole Bible.

As an example of a false personal meaning (mis)taken from Scripture, we can use an event from the life of Origen, whose dates are approximately 185–254. Origen is a Father of the Church and possibly the greatest systematic theologian in Christian history before Augustine. He belonged to the church in Alexandria. For all his merits, this saintly confessor of the faith found in Matthew 19:12 a false personal meaning. In the text, Our Lord speaks metaphorically of "eunuchs who have made themselves eunuchs for the sake of the Kingdom". Origen erroneously found here a personal invitation to have himself castrated. This mutilation is in conflict with the whole spirit of the Gospel and the Incarnation.

Precautions Against False Personal Meanings Of Scripture

If a great and holy person like Origen could make such a tragic mistake by accepting as true a blatantly false personal meaning, then ordinary people like us are certainly not immune to error. To protect ourselves against such error, we should use the whole body and spirit of Scripture as a criterion for discerning the personal meanings we find in the Bible. Whenever a personal meaning would incline us to do something unusual, we should submit our personal understanding of the Scripture text to our pastor or spiritual director for their confirmation. If our spiritual guide does not believe in the meaning we think we have found, we too should doubt it and not entrust ourselves to it. The Enemy can use even the Sacred Scriptures to try to deceive us.

Prayer During Sacred Reading

As we read Scripture, the Holy Spirit plays on the spiritual sensitivity of our souls as on a piano. The holy words are continually striking new responses from us. Today you read of the penitent woman who anointed Jesus' feet with her tears and you are filled with a holy desire for new and true repentance. Therefore, you tell God of your sorrow for the weakness and smallness of your love. Tomorrow, you read the passage where the voice comes from heaven concerning Jesus: "This is my Beloved Son in Whom I am well pleased", and suddenly you know that God is saying the same words over you. This makes you shudder. Perhaps you shed tears. You just feel so blessed. You stop your reading to

Pathways to Union with Jesus

tell God how grateful you are for His love for you. Perhaps you just praise Him for His gracious love for you. Another time you read a challenging passage like: "...whoever of you does not renounce all that he has cannot be my disciple." (Lk 14:33) These words raise some anxious doubt in you because you have not yet renounced all that you have and therefore you wonder if you are truly His disciple. So you stop reading and start praying: "Lord help me! Help me to know what you require me to renounce in order to be your disciple, and give me strength of will to renounce it. Lord, help me to do it. I want to be your disciple!"

Dear ones, we should not *decide beforehand* to talk to God about every passage we read. We just read with the attitudes and dispositions already mentioned. We read until the Holy Spirit gives us an inner urging to speak to Him about what we have read. If the text is confusing, we might feel like asking God to help us understand. If the text reveals His loving kindness, our hearts may be moved to express gratitude and praise. If the text makes us aware of our sinfulness, we may stop reading, prostrate ourselves on the floor physically (or at least spiritually in our hearts), and beg God for the grace of a new conversion. If the text "seems" to show God in a harsh light, we may feel led to ask Him about this: "Are you really an angry God?" If the text makes us aware of our sufferings in this life, we may need to complain and ask God for endurance, relief, and comfort.

Like children, in our biblical prayer we should have such implicit confidence that we can say anything to God that truly crosses our heart. This could go as far as telling God you do not like Him right now...that He demands too much...that He allows too much sin and suffering in the world...that you are angry with Him...that He *seems* unjust and uncaring. We may question God; in fact, we *must* do so, if that is what is really going on in our hearts. "Why is it this way? Why have You not answered my prayer? Cancer, infant mortality, poverty, oppression, war, violence… stupid tragic accidents that take the lives of our youth… God, don't You care? I know the wickedness of human beings and I myself am full of it. But You are an All Good God. You say You are Love. Well, what are You going to do about all this human suffering? When? How much longer do I have to see all this horrible hatred, suffering, and death? Where are You? O God, have You forsaken us? "

Dear ones, I do not want you to feel, and much less to stir up in you, these almost blasphemous emotional questionings. But if they come upon you, it is better to express them directly to God. God is big and strong. Your hurt, anger, and confusion will not wound or upset God. God wants to come to you in those feelings, so you must let them be known to God. There is no sin in this honest expression. Even saints have felt abandoned, shocked by disappointed expectations of God, wounded, terribly confused, and overwhelmed with consternation. None of those emotions should be confused with blasphemously condemning God. Hiding our negative feelings behind silence or pious words would only be hypocrisy. Let me offer some further reflections on this subject.

Reverence And Irreverence In Prayer

There is no pastoral need to convince Christians to tell their nice thoughts and feelings to God. It is easy and pleasant to do so. I am emphasizing the point that you must also tell God the negative things you feel. Blasphemous feelings (to be sharply distinguished from blasphemy in the will) come upon us all. God understands. It has to be this way. Whoever pretends otherwise is either totally insensitive to human suffering or is living in pathological denial. The unanswered questions are real. The universal sin, alienation, suffering and death go on and on. Doesn't all of that matter to us? Could we somehow not have strong dark feelings about all that? Let your confusion, hurt, and anger show. They are appropriate. They are your prayer acceptable to God.

God welcomes the expression of our blasphemous feelings. They will still be there even if we repress them from our speech or even from our consciousness. Jesus had them. He expressed them. "My God, my God, why have You forsaken me!" ...that is what Jesus experienced in His feelings, and He said it that way to His Father. In His spirit, He knew the Father was always with Him, but it did not feel that way on the cross. So it is with us. Being Christian does not mean having good devout feelings all the time. Our bad feelings are just as precious to God as our good ones. Experience shows that our negative feelings toward God are relieved by expressing them in prayer, while repressing them from prayer makes them grow more intense. How can God wipe away our tears if we do not cry in His presence? How can God answer our questions and doubts, if we do not confide them to Him? How can God assuage our hurt and anger if we keep them hidden in silence or locked in our unconscious? Honest expressions of blasphemous angry feeling by those who seek God sincerely are preferable to Him than the untrue pious declarations of the properly devout.

Remember Job. He complained bitterly about God's "unjust" rule over the world. He cursed his own birth, blamed God for injustice, called God to account, and told Him how rotten He has made the whole scheme of human life. Meanwhile Job's friends defended God on every point. In their forced reverence for God, they would say nothing negative about God and they made no complaints to Him for allowing such bad things to happen in the human world. Shockingly, God's final judgment on their words and Job's comes out in God's reprimand to the friends of Job: "My wrath is kindled against you… for you have not spoken of Me what is right, *as my servant Job has*." (Job 42:7)

It is not a good and commendable thing to speak irreverently to God. No one should ever encourage the practice for its own sake. But if, as inevitably happens at some times in every Christian life, a person does have these negative thoughts and feelings, the best thing to do is to express them honestly to ourselves and to God. Then God will deliver us from them…even as He delivered Job from his harsh words: "…I have uttered what I did not understand, things too wonderful for me, which I did not know" (Job 42:3)

Here I offer a personal experience in support of what I am saying. My mother and father did not have their lives together during the years they were raising their children. Both were alcoholics. Dad was an absentee and Mom was very much off on her own thing, leaving us kids alone a good bit. At the end of my second year of school, I was left back. That was the first time Mom took any notice of what was going on with me at school. I had to repeat the whole year. The public humiliation devastated my already weak self-confidence. It didn't help my self-esteem later that summer when it was discovered that my eyesight was so poor I could not see the writing on the black board or the printed page. Wearing thick glasses just made me feel dumber. I never fully recovered from that early social disgrace.

In my middle fifties, I told this sad story of parental neglect to some close friends. Later on that day, when I was alone, I thought about that conversation. For the first time in my life, I let myself have some of the feelings that would have been appropriate for the second grader. I began to feel terribly hurt and very angry with my mother for not taking care of me. "It was not right! It was not right! That shouldn't have happened to me! It was wrong and bad and my mother didn't care! And why did You let them do that to me, Jesus? Why weren't you there? Why didn't you take care of me? Why did you let them neglect me?" At that very moment, I had an interior vision. Jesus came right up to me. His eyes were filled with tears of compassion. He put his arms around me with my head on His chest. He kept rocking me gently in His arms, saying, "William, my William, I didn't want them to do that to you. It has never stopped hurting me that they neglected you. I am sorry, so sorry, that awful thing happened to you. It should never have happened! It was wrong and evil! All your life, every day, I have wanted to tell you how much I feel the hurts they did to you. I've been waiting for you to come to me with this pain so I could heal and comfort you. Only now, now that you are telling me your hurt, can I tell you mine. I love you, William, and I, I myself, will make it up to you a thousand time over."

Dear ones, do not be like me. Do not wait fifty years to cry out to Jesus in your hurt, anger, and confusion. When you cry out, Jesus will come.

IV CONTEMPLATION

Contemplatio. Contemplation is a wordless response of joyful loving attention to the mystery of Divine Love, Presence, and Goodness when it is experienced during sacred reading.

We simply receive God's word in *Reading*. We repeat it over and over by heart in *Meditation*. We reply to God in spontaneous words when we are visited by the spiritual gift of *Prayer*. At certain moments of grace, Jesus, The Word who reveals the Love of God, visits us. Then we reply in silence, simply knowing, loving, surrendering to, and enjoying God loving us. This is *Contemplation*.

Reading, we receive. Meditating, we receive more deeply. Praying, we respond in mental or vocal words to God. Contemplating, we respond simply by giving our loving attention to the Lord Who makes us experience His Presence and His Love. Prayer is a response of the mind, employing the flow of thoughts and words. Contemplation is a response of the heart, employing the silent flow of loving attention. Prayer expresses love in many acts of thought and word. Contemplation expresses love in one single act of intentional conscious awareness.

St. Bernard of Clairvaux (+1153) gave us an apt expression to describe the gift of contemplation given to one who is reading the Scriptures. He calls those moments of grace, "Visitations by the Word". As important as the Sacred Scriptures are, they fade into the background when Jesus makes us know His presence and His love. Once the Bible reveals

Jesus, its work is completed. It is Jesus, and not the Scriptures, Who ultimately reveals the Father to us. For "no one knows the Father except the Son and anyone to whom the Son chooses to reveal Him." (Mt 11:27b)

In Mt 28:10 and Mk 16:07, a wonderful promise is made to the disciples: They would see the Risen Lord in Galilee. All serious disciples of Jesus of every generation have desired with all their hearts to see the Lord. We wish we could go to Galilee to see Him there. That is no longer physically possible. Happily, Jesus still shows Himself, even in our time, to His disciples. He shows Himself to us in our hearts, in the community, in sacraments of faith, and in a most blessed way in Scripture. In a symbolic sense, the Sacred Scriptures are our Galilee. Jesus has gone on there before us. He waits for us there. We must go to Galilee, to the Scriptures, and there we will see Him. This is a fulfillment of His promise to come to us and make his home with us. (Jn 14:21-23)

Description Of Scriptural Contemplation

First let us clear up any obscurity about what we mean in the present context by this word of many meanings, "contemplation". Here follows a suggestive illustration taken from everyday life. Let us say a beautiful flower, or a sunset, or a magnificent full moon has caught your attention. During the first seconds of your attention to that beauty, you do not think or say anything. You simply see, know, love, appreciate, and enjoy the beauty you are beholding. That is the kind of contemplation we are talking about. It is not catatonic rapture or "out of the body" ecstasy. It involves no loss of consciousness or of self-dominion. It is a simple, personal act of delightful awareness of God's love, goodness, and beauty present to you.

If natural and visible things of beauty have the power to catch us up into contemplation, the supernatural and invisible things of God have far greater power to enrapture us. Now, therefore, we can offer this definition: *Contemplation is the gift of illumined consciousness and heightened awareness of the Presence of God loving us.* This awareness arises within us as a strong impression of God's Presence and His personal love for us here and now.

The final purpose of the creation of the universe, the whole intention of God in all of Scriptures, and the ultimate goal of the entire history of Salvation, all come down to this one thing: God is making us know Himself: Divine Love, Goodness, Beauty, and Truth. God The Word, Jesus, is the Divine Agent,

Pathways to Union with Jesus

the Medium, and the Object of this blessed knowledge. The purpose, therefore, of all *things* in nature and in grace is this: to reveal God, to reveal God's Love for us, in and through Jesus. "No one knows the Father except the Son and anyone to whom the Son chooses to reveal him." (Mt 11:27b)

By little and little, we come to grasp God's love for us. We hear about it in preaching, read about it in scripture and other books, and we feel some suggestion of it in Nature. However, as we are reading, meditating, or praying over the Scriptures, it sometimes happens that we suddenly feel overwhelmingly aware of God's Presence and His Love. This is a "visitation by the Word". Jesus has come. He is making you know the Father, as only He is able.

In the biblical contemplation of which we speak, a perceptible spiritual mood comes upon us. We never know when it will descend upon us, how long it will remain, or when it will leave. It is recognizable as a unique sweetness, a joy in the heart that rushes like a mountain steam with laughter in its coursing waters. The corporeal eyes see nothing. The ears hear nothing. But the eyes of the heart see Him. And our spiritual ears hear Him sing His love to us. Our hearts glow within us while He silently speaks to us. Our soul feels His Presence. And we rejoice with exceeding great joy at this sight of the Lord. Galilee!

You may be reading a passage of profound depth such as Jn 19:30 where Jesus, hanging on the cross for our salvation, says: "It is finished. And He bowed His head and gave up His Spirit". As you read these words God might raise your awareness of what it means that "God so loved the World…" yes, and so loved you, "…that He gave His only Son, that whoever believes in him should not perish but have eternal life." (Jn 3:16) The powerful awareness could hold your attention still for a time fixed in joyful contemplation.

When the light of biblical contemplation comes upon you, God inhabits your awareness so that you know by experience the love you are reading about in Scripture. The Divine Lover, loving you, is present. You feel it. You enjoy it, perhaps with holy tears. Now you stop reading, stop meditating, stop praying. You just gaze upon the Love that is surrounding you and filling you. You do nothing, for now, but know the Lord. You receive the Gift He is. You taste the Goodness He is. You know the Truth He is. You enjoy the Beauty He is. You are surrendering your whole being to the One who is giving Himself to you. While Jesus the Word "visits" you

Pathways to Union with Jesus

in contemplation, you can do nothing else but be a lovingly attentive host. This is the "one thing necessary" and you are fully occupied in knowing, loving, and enjoying the Word in His visitation.

The "visitation" of the Word in biblical contemplation may come upon us when we are reading seemingly unimportant passages of Scripture. Jn 4:06 is an introductory descriptive verse which merely states that, "Jesus, wearied as He was with His journey, sat down beside the well". A verse as simple as this picture of Jesus may become the spark of sublime contemplation. The image of God-made-man, tired out from seeking sinners along the dusty roads of this wayward world, might strike a person into awareness of the immensity and the immanence of God's love, so that she might not be able to go on reading, but is held by the engrossing awareness.

One man was about to begin reading the Gospel of Mark. At the head of the page in the upper margin, before the inspired text began in the old edition he was using, there was a title added by the printer. This was not even Scripture, it was just a phrase printed at the top of the page by some modern printer or editor. It said: "The Holy Gospel of Our Lord and Savior Jesus Christ according to

Mark". The man read that phrase and was taken by it. He read it again, and again. It penetrated his soul and caused him to weep at the awesome meaning of the words. Finally, these precious words lifted him to an intense awareness of the Love of God in silent contemplation.

I heard of another example. A man was accustomed to seeking the Lord in lectio every day at the same early hour. One day he went to the usual place at the accustomed hour and picked up the Bible. He had not yet settled down and was still in a distracted mood. Suddenly, the feel of the Holy Book in his hands, and the sight of it in front of his eyes, gave him a most profound and powerful consciousness of God and of God's love coming upon him. Tears began to flow and he was immediately swept into total awareness of the Love which had now become present and manifest to him. Simply to look at the Bible is enough to cause us to fall into contemplation! If God so wills.

When the attraction to gaze upon the Beloved in contemplation wanes, we should not try to hold on to it. Rather, we should simply return to our reading of the Holy Word. As the Spirit educates us, we will learn to move with lightness and grace back and forth, from reading to contemplation and back to reading; from reading to meditation or to prayer and back again to reading.

Desire the spiritual gift of contemplation. Ask for it, but do not *try* to get it. That would be spiritual selfishness. When it comes, enjoy it fully. When it leaves, have no regrets. Always prefer the everyday work of sacrificial love even to the most exalted contemplation. If you must choose between this contemplative delight and the duty of love, choose the duty. God will be more present in your responsible decision than in your delightful vision.

We have an example of this in the monk who literally walked out on a vision of Christ in Glory in his cell when the bell rang calling him to distribute food to the poor. Christ was still present and waiting for the monk when he returned from doing his duty of love. And Jesus said to him: "If thou had stayed I would have fled."

Of all the things I have ever read or learned about prayer and contemplation, I consider the following statement to have the most fundamental importance and far reaching implications. *When God gives us any momentary conscious experience of spiritual bliss He intends to strengthen our permanent faith that we have all of the same spiritual blessings from God at every moment of our lives.* Christians live by the enduring experience of faith, not by the fleeting experience of conscious blissful contemplation.

The gift of sacrificial love is vastly greater than the greatest gift of blessed contemplation. Contemplation may increase your love. Welcome contemplation but make love your aim. (1Cor 13: 1 – 13)

The Goal Of Lectio Divina: Agape

The final—and absolutely necessary—fruit of lectio divina and of all authentic contemplative prayer is growth in sacrificial love for the people God places in our lives. This growth in effective love for others proves the spiritual quality of our life of sacred reading and contemplative prayer. Without this increase in agape, our prayer and contemplation would have to be judged false, valueless, and self-indulgent illusion. The deeds of love are the seeds of contemplative knowledge of God, and true contemplation bears fruit in deeds of love. Amen.

TO THE PATHWAY OF
THE JESUS PRAYER

Lectio Divina And The Jesus Prayer

In a profound sense, all the words of Scripture are summed up in the one Word: Jesus. The revelation God gives us in scripture is intended to bring us sinners to repentance, asking God for the fullness of His mercy in the Name of Jesus.

The Jesus Prayer is a condensation of all scriptures and of all human response to the revealed Word of God. In fewer words or in more, salvation from God follows upon the sinners prayer of the heart: "Lord Jesus Christ, Son of God, have mercy on me, a sinner."

A sacrament is a sign that makes present what it signifies. The word of scripture is a sacrament of Jesus, the Word of God. Union with Jesus, the Word of God, in lectio divina, transforms our heart (the source of our emotions) and our mind (the source of our thoughts). Union with Jesus in the Jesus Prayer gives life, light, and love to our personal spirits (the source of our free choices). In the Jesus Prayer, we concentrate on one word of scripture, the one Word that fulfills the meaning of all of the other words in the bible. The Word is Jesus. The Jesus Prayer is also called, "The Prayer of the Heart," or, "Breath Prayer" for reasons that will be made clear in the next chapter.

# CHAPTER THREE

THE PATHWAY OF THE JESUS PRAYER

Pathways to Union with Jesus

THE JESUS PRAYER

Jesus And Prayer

The first seven verses of the 15th Chapter of the Gospel of John present us with the image of Jesus as the True Vine and of His followers as His branches. These verses promise that the Christian who abides in Him will bear much fruit. We bear fruit inwardly by spiritual transformation and outwardly by deeds of love. All fruit-bearing depends on "abiding." As an expression of simple faith in Christ, and as a spiritual manner of eating and drinking of His flesh and blood, the Jesus Prayer is an utterly simple and exceedingly profound way of abiding in Jesus in a personal relationship. Far from being merely a formal discipline of prayer, practice of the Jesus Prayer leads to continual transforming union with Jesus in the heart and in our works of love in the world.

The Jesus Prayer, also known as the "Prayer of the Heart", is an expression of personal faith in Jesus Christ as Son of God and Savior of the World. The believer focuses her or his conscious loving attention on the Person of the Lord Jesus while calling upon Him for the fullness of personal and universal salvation.

Defining The Jesus Prayer

It is not simply a mechanical repetition of a sacred formula. The Jesus Prayer is a continually repeated *personal act of loving attention* to Jesus. It is an act of conscious attention to the Lord Jesus, gazing upon Him by faith full of love, desire, holy sorrow, ineffable delight, and invincible trust.

The essential element of this prayer is *invocation of God:* a human person calls to the divine Person by name. Any biblical substantive that refers to God may be used, such as, Lord, Jesus, Christ, Son of God, Beloved, Savior, Redeemer, etc. Because the Father and the Son are One God in the Spirit, it really doesn't matter which Divine Person you call upon. They are in each other. Down through the history of salvation, however, God the Father has drawn the world, every person, to the Son through the Spirit. The Son gathers us into Himself and takes us to the Father in the same Spirit.

The classical formula that has been preserved in constant use to this day in the Orthodox Church is (with minor variations): "*O Lord Jesus Christ, Son of God, have mercy on me a sinner*". Since the rise of the cult of the saints during the middle ages, popular devotion has inserted into this formula a reference to Mary, the Mother of the Lord. Some Eastern Christians find this addition to be helpful. Others find it to be a distracting accretion to the older form, which focuses on Jesus alone. Make your own choice.

The classical formula is composed of two Gospel elements. The first half, "Lord Jesus Christ, Son of God…" recalls the words of the blind beggar, Bartimaeus: "Jesus, Son of David, have mercy on me!" (Mark 10: 47) The classical formula of the Jesus Prayer amplifies Bartimaeus' words in the light of Christian faith that Jesus is not only son of David but Son of God.

The second part of the classical formula, "…have mercy on me a sinner", expresses the humility and sincerity of the tax collector at prayer in the Temple: "God, be merciful to me a sinner!" (Luke 18:13) Our blessed Lord presented this example tor us to follow. Whatever verbal formula is used, the Jesus Prayer should be offered with the irrepressible faith of Bartimaeus and the tax collector's humble confession of our sinful human condition asking for God's mercy.

The Name of Jesus is the center of all forms of the Jesus Prayer. Some of the shorter formulas that have come down to us are: "God be merciful to me a sinner"; "Lord have mercy"; "Lord Jesus have mercy". The simplest forms consist in calling upon the Name, "Lord Jesus," or just: "Jesus". Let us review the meaning of the Blessed Name to enrich our prayer. **The Meaning Of The Name Of Jesus**

Components: The first part, "Je-" of the English name "Je-sus" derives from an abbreviation of the Hebrew Sacred Tetragrammaton, YHWH, transliterated as Yahweh. "Yahweh" is the personal name of God revealed to Moses at the burning bush: "I AM". The last part of Jesus' name, "-sus" in English, is a derivative of the Hebrew word, "SHUA," meaning "SALVATION." The name of Jesus, therefore, means something like, "Salvation from Yahweh" or "Yahweh is Salvation." According to Matthew 1: 21, God willed that the Child to be born must be named Jesus "because He will save His people from their sins."

What We Ask For In The Jesus Prayer

Christian prayer must never be an expression of alienated egocentric self-interest. We do indeed pray explicitly for ourselves and for those entrusted to our love. Implicitly, however, we want every other human being to have the good things we pray for personally. When we call upon the Lord Jesus, using

Pathways to Union with Jesus

any formula, it should be our implicit intention to ask God to give all of God's goodness to all of God's creation. Even though we may use the first person singular pronoun in the formula or just one single word, like "Lord" or "Jesus", let us agree to desire all of God's gifts for all of God's creatures. The Jesus Prayer is meant to be a universal all-inclusive prayer, asking for everything good for every human being, beginning with the one who prays.

In praying the Jesus Prayer, we must remember in faith that Jesus is the one Gift of God Who contains in Himself our deliverance from *all* evil and in Him we receive *every* good thing that God can give -beyond all we could think or desire. "Jesus" is the name of all the grace, goodness, life, love, and happiness that God has to give to the whole created universe. In this sense, the name of Jesus is a universal prayer of petition. Whoever wants Jesus in prayer wants the end of all sin, evil, suffering, and death in her/his own life and in the life of every human being. At the same time, whoever wants Jesus in prayer wants the infinite, eternal, plenitude of all the blessings of grace and glory from God upon him/herself and upon the whole of creation. The Jesus Prayer asks for all of the blessings that God has to give to come upon all that God has made.

Pathways to Union with Jesus

There are two complimentary ways of praying the Jesus Prayer: *continual* and *formal*.

The Continual Use Of The Jesus Prayer

In the continual use of the Prayer, we try to remember Jesus with love and trust frequently during the day in the midst of our engagements. Here follow some suggestions to help form the habit of practicing the Jesus Prayer continually.

Whenever we become aware of any troubling thought or feeling inside us we can cover it, as with anointing oil, with an act of loving trust in Jesus. That is, we replace every anxiety, fear, doubt, sadness, pain, sorrow, or desire by invoking Jesus with love and trust. Whatever needs to happen, He will do it. Similarly, whenever we become aware of somebody else in need or suffering, or when we see the possibility for more life and happiness crying out for fulfillment in the lives of others, we can invoke Jesus. We can habitually call on Jesus who satisfies all human need, takes away all suffering, and fulfills all of the possibilities for more love, more life, and more happiness of every creature.

If we have faith, we experience the real presence of Jesus when we call upon His Name with love. A Christian can bring Jesus into any place or situation at any time by the simple loving invocation of His Name.

"Your name is oil poured out", the Beloved says to her Lover (Song of Solomon, 1: 03). In ancient Israel, oil was poured out to nourish as food, to give light as lamp fuel, to heal as oil of anointing, and to consecrate as king and Priest. Calling upon the Name of Jesus, nourishes, enlightens, heals, and consecrates us in the royal priesthood of Christ.

The Priestly Blessing Of The Jesus Prayer

In the book of Numbers, Chapter 6, verses 22-27, God commanded the priests to bless the people by putting God's Name upon them: "put my name on the Israelites and I will bless them." We who have been baptized into the priesthood of the Risen Christ (1Pt 2:9) are the fulfillment of what was dimly foreshadowed by the priesthood of Aaron. How much more fitting is it, then, that every Christian should continually "put the Name" of all blessing upon the people. We can, indeed we should, make it our priestly practice to put the Name of Jesus upon our loved ones, and upon the people we meet in our daily life—especially those in need, sorrow, or trouble, and those who offend us. Pour out the oil of

Jesus' Name upon them that they may be nourished, enlightened, healed, and consecrated to God. Love those who have been entrusted to you in family and friendship by anointing them with the Name of Jesus in the sanctuary of your heart. How better could we bless our loved ones—and our enemies—than by putting the Name of Jesus upon them?

Both we ourselves and the other persons will be blessed if we call upon Jesus on their behalf. It is a joy to "put the Name of Jesus" on a person for whom we feel affection, compassion, gratitude, or loving concern. The mutual blessing will be even greater if we choose to put all the goodness of Jesus upon persons who do not love us, person who stir in us judgmental thoughts or the negative emotions of impatience, anger, jealousy, or fear.

Put the Name on your children as they go to bed. Cover your spouse in the Name before you fall asleep together and in the morning when you part for work. When you remember someone you love do not just think of him or her. Bless them with all blessing from afar by invoking the Name of Jesus upon them.

We cannot always *feel* a desire for all goodness for the other person but we can always *choose* to want it. By choice and decision, we can want for the person upon whom we "put the Name" all of the love and gifts of grace God wants to give to that person in Jesus. The next time you are offended by a rude driver, instead of letting road rage take over, try invoking the Name of Jesus upon the offender. He will be blessed without even knowing you prayed for him and you will feel much better.

Method For The Formal Use Of The Jesus Prayer

Before we go into the details about methods that can be used in a formal practice of the Jesus Prayer, I would like to clear up a question that frequently arises. Is the Christian Jesus Prayer the same thing as a Hindu mantra? Actually, the similarities are as immediately noticeable as they are purely superficial. The repetition of a sacred formula is common and both activities produce comparable beneficial physical and psychological effects, such as stress reduction, lower blood pressure, slower heart rate, mental tranquility, etc. The similarity ends with these externals.

Notice these differences: The meaning of the mantra in Eastern practice has no importance. The meaning of the Jesus Prayer is of infinite importance.

Pathways to Union with Jesus

A mantra is used to empty the mind. The Jesus Prayer fills the heart, mind, and spirit with the presence of God. The mantra is a yoga-discipline practiced by an individual in himself or herself. The Jesus Prayer is an inter-personal relationship of love that unites the Person of Jesus with the person who prays.

Above all, the intention of the one who uses the formula distinguishes the two traditions. A Christian uses the Jesus Prayer as an act of personal faith and love for Jesus. It is an act of self-surrender to God and a humble petition for complete spiritual healing and wholeness for oneself and for the whole world. Mantras have nothing of this.

Understanding how the Jesus Prayer is unique among religious practices in the world, let us now consider the details of method for its formal practice.

Scriptural Foundations

We have received the Jesus Prayer from tradition that goes as far back as Bartimaeus, before the New Testament was written. But our forebears in Christ developed this prayer strictly from biblical sources. So must we.

Prayer Of The Heart

What is the heart? Where is that place inside us where we offer the Jesus Prayer? One's "heart" is ones inner self, one's personal spirit that is being breathed forth and sustained in being by God. The heart is the person: the spiritual agent of consciousness, free choice, intention, and attention. The "heart" is what we most deeply mean by the pronoun "I". Out of this inner person, the heart, proceed good thoughts or evil ones according to our choice to accept or disown them. Out of the heart flows the choice and the act of giving one's loving attention to Jesus in the prayer of calling on His Name.

The Faith Foundation Of The Jesus Prayer

If you can appropriate the following confession, then you have the prerequisite faith foundation necessary to offer the Jesus Prayer.

I believe that:

- According to His promise, Jesus has come and made His home in me.

- Jesus abides in me and I in Him, united like a Vine and a branch.

Pathways to Union with Jesus

- He is with me always, every minute, even to the end of time and forever.

- Christ dwells in my heart through faith.

- I truly know the Lord, even though He transcends my understanding.

- In knowing Jesus, I know the God's Love incarnate.

- I have immediate access to Jesus in my heart at all times in faith.

- The Spirit empowers me to give my personal conscious attention to Him.

- My mustard seed of faith is enough to experience Jesus in me.

- The Father is drawing me to the Son when I offer the Jesus Prayer.

- Only by the power of the Spirit do I call to Jesus in Person.

If you did not believe these things, your offering of the Jesus Prayer would be hollow pretense and meaningless fiction. If you have faith, though as small as a mustard seed, all things are possible.

Details Of Practice: Choosing A Place And Time

The remembrance of Jesus-God is Life-giving. We want our awareness of God to become habitual to our life. So that, whenever our minds are not occupied in dong the works God appoints for us, our hearts and thoughts revert to awareness of God. Otherwise, our conscious attention will be wasted on temporal things that have no eternal value, worldly things that do not give us Life. In order to establish the Jesus Prayer as a continual habit of the heart, it is helpful to dedicate fifteen to thirty minutes each day to practicing it in a conscious formal manner. Triply blessed will you be if you set time aside for the Jesus Prayer in the morning and in the evening.

If you dedicate a certain time and a special place where you habitually devote yourself to the Jesus Prayer, that time and place will become like angels of God inviting you into God's presence. When you fail to appear before God in prayer in the consecrated place and time you have set apart, that special place and time will call you to repent and return to the Lord.

Pathways to Union with Jesus

If you choose a special chair or use a certain posture that you take only when you pray, those material things likewise will incline your heart and mind to prayer.

Before praying, assume the dispositions of Bartimaeus and the tax collector. Like Bartimaeus, come to Jesus as one drawn to Him by God the Father with irrepressible urgency and absolute certainty that Jesus can and will heal you and make you whole according to your need. Like the tax collector, come before God in the Jesus Prayer with humble awareness of your moral failures and the incompleteness of your love. Enter God's presence, by means of this prayer, depending and trusting completely that the God of endless mercy will hear and answer your prayer.

If you wish, you can use the rhythm of your heartbeat or your breathing as a means to begin the Jesus Prayer. The Jesus Prayer is called the "Prayer of the Heart" because it is with the heart that faith sees, loves, and desires Jesus. If you wish, you can teach your heart to say the Name of Jesus or any other formula of the Jesus Prayer. In ordinary conventional speech, we associate the meaning of an idea or an intention with a particular sound we make with our voice. We can intentionally mean "Jesus" and attend to Him as we associate His Name (or other words of a Jesus Prayer formula) with the repetitive contraction and relaxation of our cardiac muscle. One does this by mentally pronouncing the prayer word(s) with each beat-rest motion of the heart. Soon the practitioner can just "listen" to her or his heart saying the Jesus Prayer.

The practice of associating the words of the Jesus Prayer formula with the rhythm of breathing has given rise to referring to it as "Breath Prayer". While Inhaling, one can silently say, "O Lord Jesus Christ, Son of God…" While exhaling, one can say, "…have mercy on me a sinner." One person whom I know says, "Jesus" while inhaling. He thinks of himself as inhaling the Breath of Life, Jesus, the Word eternally breathed forth by the Father. Then, filled with the Life-giving Breath of God, he returns to God the Father with Jesus crying "Abba" while exhaling.

My practice has evolved becoming simpler over my lifetime. With each breath I take and release, I associate the two sacred words, "Lord Jesus" or just the two syllables of the Holy Name, Je-sus.

When you come to the time and place set aside for prayer, let it be as solitary and quiet as possible. Be creative if your circumstances make it difficult to

Pathways to Union with Jesus

be alone and silent. One family man takes refuge in a small closet kept empty for this purpose. Another father of young children gets up half an hour before the daily family life begins. Someone else goes out and sits in his car in order to find thirty minutes of silence and solitude.

When you sit to pray, close your eyes. Take a few exceptionally deep breaths and exhale fully and slowly. As you release your breath, consciously relax into the loving providence of God. Intentionally let your mind and your muscles relax. God is taking care of all of the things you are concerned about. At least now, let Him carry all of your burdens. Trust God, your almighty Protector and Provider.

The few deep breaths will settle down your heart rate, lower your blood pressure, and slow the racing of your thoughts. Then breath normally, keeping your eyes closed. Begin praying with whatever formula of invocation you prefer. For the purpose of example, I will use my personal favorite short formula of the Jesus Prayer, simply: "Lord Jesus". Gently inhaling, look at Him and call to Him in your heart, that is, in your personal spirit: "Lord". Peacefully exhaling, complete your invocation with the Name above all names: "Jesus". Repeat the prayer with every breath.

Pathways to Union with Jesus

The prayer is an act of conscious loving attention to Jesus in Person. As you are inclined and as you are able, fill your awareness of Him with all the love you have. If you can feel your love of Christ, that is a blessing. If you cannot feel any emotion of love, then just desire to love Him in your free will. That desire is enough. Anyone who desires to love Jesus *already loves Him* even if there are no feelings of affection.

As you pray, do not stir up your fears, cares, and hopes but allow them to arise on their own. As they appear in your consciousness, without mulling over them, just place them under the universal Jesus Prayer you are offering. Jesus Whom you are invoking in your prayer is God's answer to all our sorrows, fears, concerns, hopes and joys. More words of petition are unnecessary and they would clutter your thoughts and distract your loving attention to Jesus.

God, One and Triune, is the only Receiver of all Christian prayer. Therefore, it is essentially the same as the Jesus Prayer, if one calls upon God the Father or God the Holy Spirit. The three Persons of the Trinity dwell within each other. "Trinity" (trinitas in Latin) means "threeness"; it does not mean "three" as a number of separate beings. Therefore a Christian has the liberty to invoke the only True God

Pathways to Union with Jesus

by any Name He has used of Himself in Scripture. Let the Spirit lead you, personally. In my personal journey, I have always felt drawn by the Spirit to Jesus as the Way to the Father. And over time, I have increasingly learned to delight in calling out to God, my "Abba Father".

If the heartbeat or the breathing cycle is used as a vehicle for prayer, it is important not to allow these physical methods to interfere with your attention to God while you pray. It takes some effort and attention to establish these methods as habits. Once established, they should be put out of our consciousness so that we can attend fully and only to the One Whom we are invoking in our prayer. At the beginning of our formal time of prayer it helps to focus on the rhythm our heart or our breath in order to establish a rhythm in calling upon the Lord. Once our loving attention is fixed upon the Lord, we should forget about our physical breathing and our heartbeat. Unnecessary attention to heart or breath would be a distraction.

When thoughts spontaneously arise and distract us from our attention to God in prayer, which is certain to occur, we may return to the rhythm of our breathing or heartbeat as a means of re-centering our attention upon God. Once we are again attentive to God, we should give only as much attention as is necessary to the physical aspects of our respiration or heartbeat.

The method of using the heart or breath to get started in prayer may be compared to a jet on the runway of an airport. The runway (the method) is very important until the plane leaves the ground. At that point the runway has served its purpose and is now superfluous. It is left behind. Likewise, as soon as we are soaring in loving attention to Jesus, we should forget the rhythm of our breath or physical heartbeat.

It is important to note these two elements of the Jesus Prayer: *attention*, and *affection*. In this prayer, we give to Jesus conscious attention with love and holy desire. We are not trying to empty the mind but to fill it with the One Thing Necessary. We are not trying to eliminate the affection of the heart but to direct all of it to the One Beloved. We are not trying to extinguish desires but to unify them by placing all of our desire upon the one Gift of God, Jesus.

Know that the Jesus Prayer is not a fixed mental state. It is not experienced as resting on a plateau or as a sustained higher state of consciousness. It is indeed good to be there, but we cannot build tabernacles to remain there permanently. The Jesus Prayer is rightly understood—using an image borrowed from St. Augustine—as the flight of an arrow. Its nature is fleeting rather than permanent, repetitive rather than continuous. Its value does not lie in the length of time it remains fixed upon the mark without distraction. Do not waste energy trying to "hold" your contemplative gaze. When our contemplative attention is prolonged, it happens by the grace of God and not by our effort to concentrate. The value of the Jesus Prayer lies in the sincerity and directness with which it is uttered in each fleeting repetition. In the Jesus Prayer, the *quality* of the arrow's flight is what matters most. Let it flow sincerely from our heart aimed directly to God. Let the arrows of prayer fly—as many as we have.

How many times should we repeat our formula of prayer? The number is totally irrelevant. Just repeat the prayer, without counting, as long as your prayer time lasts. Considered as an act of contemplation, we repeat the prayer just to be consciously, lovingly, aware of Him. Considered as a universal prayer of petition, our Lord fully answers our prayer the first time we utter it.

How To Deal With Distractions

It is natural for the mind to change the focus of its attention continually, incessantly. You should expect to lose the focus of your attention upon Jesus in a matter of seconds or a few minutes at most. Those distractions do not disqualify your prayer. They are sufferings you are to endure with patience and with compassion upon yourself. All hell has broken lose in attacking you. More than anything else, demons hate Christians who are lovingly attentive to Jesus. The distractions they sow in your mind are not sins but only temptations. Do not blame yourself for them. They happen as involuntary experiences, not moral choices. However, what you choose to do after you become aware of a distraction is of uttermost importance.

When you call upon Jesus in the Prayer you will become consciously aware of Him for a short time. You repeat the invocation and your loving attention again reaches the Lord Who dwells within you. After a matter or minutes, you will likely find yourself thinking about something else. The great enemy of conscious attention to another person is *thinking.* Distractions are a fall from giving loving attention to His Person into thinking. When you become aware of this change from attention to thinking, you are presented with a choice: either to continue your mental engagement with the distracting thoughts or to return to the act of loving attention to Jesus. If you decide to put the distracting thoughts aside in order to return to your loving awareness of Jesus, blessed are you! It is as if you said—and you might well say: "Lord Jesus, I find myself thinking about other things. But I prefer to give my loving attention to you. I set aside all these thoughts because I would rather gaze upon you in loving attention." Then you return to your heart or breathe and renew the Prayer of loving attention to Jesus. Your free decision to discontinue a line of distracting thought in order to "return to the Lord" in love is a beautiful deed done to the Lord. It gives God joy to be chosen and preferred by you in this way above all things and all thoughts. God will reward you with sevenfold blessing. "In returning and rest you shall be saved…" (Isa 3015)

The Jesus Prayer And The Gospel Paradigm Of Salvation

If you examine the Gospel narratives, you will discover this pattern: Certain persons feel drawn to Jesus. Somehow they know, without knowing how they know, that He is good and worthy of their trust. These people have an unproven certainty that Jesus both can and will answer their prayer. Bartimaeus knows that Jesus will give him sight. A pagan Syro-Phenician woman is so sure that Jesus can and will deliver her child that she overcomes the initial hesitancy of Jesus by her humble insistence and prevails upon Him to grant her request. So great was her faith! A leper broke the law by falling at Jesus feet asking to be cleansed of his disease. A penitent sinful woman was so sure of Jesus' love that she entered the home of a Pharisee who despised her in order to weep over His feet and wipe away the tears with her hair. A woman with a flow of blood had such confidence in Jesus that she literally stole a healing from Him by touching the fringe of His garment with faith. Other biblical examples could be added. Of all of them we ask, "Where did these people get their faith in Jesus?" They got it in the same way and from the same source that anyone who prays the Jesus Prayer gets it, namely, as a gift from God the Father. No one in the time of Jesus' earthly life, and no one today, can come to Jesus, believing that He can and will grant them the desire of their heart, unless God the Father draws the person. (Jn 6:44) We practice the Jesus Prayer, not as from ourselves alone, but because the Father sends the Spirit Who draws and empowers us to call upon the Name. (1Cor 12:3)

This is the pattern of salvation: the Father draws a person to the Son inspiring full confidence that Jesus has the power and the love to do the good thing that is asked of Him. When a person prays the Jesus Prayer, she or he is being drawn to the Son by the Father through the Spirit. With confidence given from above the one who prays trusts that Jesus can and will do the good thing that is asked of Him because He has the power and the love to do so.

Fruits Of The Jesus Prayer

The Fruit of Union. The first, last, and greatest fruit of practicing the Jesus Prayer is the personal union we have with Him in the prayer itself. Jesus already and always dwells in our spirit, but when we pray, calling to Him, "Lord Jesus", we become consciously and intentionally aware of Him in the present time and place of our body and soul.

The Fruit of Transformation. As we give our personal attention to Jesus in the prayer, we become increasingly like Him. Remember, our personal spirit is like a mirror. It takes on the likeness of what is set before it. While we offer the Jesus Prayer, our spirit gazes upon Jesus with love. His image impresses itself in ever greater depth and detail upon our spirit. This happens because God "has shone in our hearts to give the light of the knowledge of the glory of God in the face of Jesus Christ." (2 Cor 4:6) "And we all, with unveiled face, beholding the glory of the Lord, are being transformed into the same image from one degree of glory to another." (2 Cor 3:18)

The Fruit of Love. The on-going transformation of our inner person through our contemplation of Jesus in the Prayer strengthens our spirit in love in all that we think, speak, and do in the world. Progressively transformed by the power of the Name of Jesus, we become increasingly empowered to transform the world through our deeds of love. All thanks and glory be to God Alone!

TO THE PATHWAY OF DISCERNMENT OF THOUGHTS

We have now completed our study two time-honored pathways to union with Jesus: **Lectio Divina** and the **Jesus Prayer**. In the next chapter we will study a pathway that is not practiced as a devotional exercise for short intermittent periods of time. Discernment of thoughts is a continuous moral consciousness. Discernment is the queen of all moral virtues because it alone enables us to receive all the other spiritual gifts of God while defending us from subtle temptations. By discernment we say "yes" to every gift sent from heaven and "no" to every deceit offered by hell. The gift of discernment clarifies our spiritual perception, enabling us to recognize God's will for our lives and His Presence in our hearts. Discernment enables us to perceive God's Self-Revelation in our Lectio Divina and in our Jesus Prayer. Discernment of thoughts purifies the heart. And blessed are those who attain to "love that issues from a pure heart". (1 Tim 1:5)

CHAPTER FOUR

THE PATHWAY OF DISCERNMENT OF THOUGHTS

DISCERNMENT OF THOUGHTS

Introduction

This is Eternal Life: to know the only true God and Jesus, the Messiah, Whom God the Father has sent. We know God in this life by the experience of faith. We will know God in the Life to come in the beatific vision of Jesus in His Glory, face to face. Blessed are the pure in heart for they shall see God. In this temporal life, the pure of heart know God in the mirror of faith. Our ability to see God is proportional to the purity of our hearts. The practice of discernment of thoughts purifies our hearts. In this chapter, I will pass on the oldest Christian tradition concerning discernment.

Section One presents some basic principles for *Understanding Discernment*. Section Two gives practical advise for *Practicing Discernment* and explains the mutual relationship between the *divine gift and the human practice* of discernment. Section Three, *Discerning The Will of God,* raises the subject of discernment to a higher level by answering the question: How can we discern the particular gifts of God and His inspirations in our hearts?

ONE: UNDERSTANDING DISCERNMENT

Before we can recognize and live by impulses of the Holy Spirit, we must first learn to protect ourselves from being led astray by evil thoughts. Initially, therefore, discernment is our moral defense system against *evil thoughts*.

What is an evil thought? An evil thought is anything in our mind or heart that does not conform to the truth and love of God that are revealed in Christ Jesus. These are thoughts that turn us away from goodness, truth, love, and life.

The Fathers of the Desert applied our Lord's parable of the weeds (Matthew 13: 24) to their struggle with evil thoughts. Our hearts are like fields ready to receive seed-thoughts. God is the Owner who sows good seed (thoughts and impulses of truth and love). Satan and all evil spirits are the enemy who sow the weeds: thoughts and impulses contrary to God's truth and love.

Within the limits set by God for our protection, demons can sow their evil thoughts directly by themselves. When human beings consciously or unconsciously allow Satan to use them, they become intermediate sowers of evil thoughts. Drug dealers, for instance, sow evil thoughts in peoples' hearts. We ourselves become instruments of the demons by sowing unbelieving, unloving thoughts in our own hearts or in the hearts of others.

Evil spirits are always present and involved in the sowing of an evil thought, directly, or indirectly through the ignorance or malice of human instruments. The demons passionately desire our spiritual death, which they try to bring about by sowing evil thoughts in our hearts. Evil thoughts are potential spiritual disasters for us and the enemy spirits always want them to ruin our lives. Evil thoughts always reveal the presence evil spirits. Therefore, discernment of thoughts is discernment of spirits.

Frequently repeated submission to an evil impulse gradually enslaves us. At first, evil thoughts do not have independent power over us to make us their slaves. Using our free will, we have to accept, believe, and entrust ourselves to an evil thought before it can have power over us, a power that increases every time we surrender to it. At its first sowing in our hearts, an evil thought is not yet a sin. It is only a suggestion, opportunity, or inclination to sin. An evil thought becomes a sin at the moment we voluntarily agree with it and make it our own by choice. When we agree with an evil thought, it changes us into itself. The thought of murder, agreed with, makes us murderers. The thought of adultery, freely entertained, makes us adulterers. By our acceptance, the evil thought becomes flesh and dwells in us. When we submit our freedom to an evil thought, we voluntarily become possessed by the evil thought and by the evil spirit behind it. We freely make ourselves obedient slaves to the Evil One and our bodies become his instruments for producing evil and death in the world.

EVIL THOUGHTS DEFINED

Comprehensively described, *an evil thought is any mental, moral, emotional, intellectual, psychological, or social influence that attracts, invites, suggests, or inclines a person to think or act contrary to the Truth and Love of God revealed in Jesus Christ.*

Evil thoughts can take innumerable forms, such as erroneous ideas, imaginations, pride, anger, fear, prejudices, moods, errors of judgment, false assumptions, psychological wounds, addictions, dreams, fantasies, memories, desires of our natural appetites; the allurements of sin, sex, pleasure, power, wealth, fame, success; the false values and the low moral standards our society presents to us, etc.

Evil thoughts separate a person from God. They are the original form of all sin. They are the first cause of death, both of the soul and of the body. No evil is done in the world that was not first a thought in the heart.

Thoughts sown in our hearts by the Evil Spirit have no power of their own. They are empty deceits without substance. We give power to the evil thoughts by believing them and entrusting ourselves to them. Evil thoughts are always subtle lies, typically in the form of a partial truth. They promise or imply satisfaction and happiness. They deliver shame, alienation, guilt, fear, despair, and death. They kill us if we believe them, just as Satan's original evil thought brought death to Adam and Eve when they trusted in it. They kill us by supplanting the Life-giving thoughts of truth and love sown by the Spirit.

Free and voluntary acceptance of an evil thought is already sin, even if it is never carried out in any external action. Our Blessed Lord taught this, using the act of adultery as a concrete example of a universal truth for all sin: "...everyone who looks at a woman *to desire her* (italicized words literally translate the original Greek: προς το επιθυμεσαι αυτην) has already committed adultery with her in his heart."

(Mt 5:28) The same is true for the desire of greed, pride, envy, violence, etc. If you freely desire to do evil in your heart, you have already done it there.

The first appearance in our consciousness of an evil attraction, be it for a sexual act, a place of honor, wealth, a material possession, a position of power, fame, etc, is not a sin. It becomes a sin when we accept the evil attraction and make it out chosen desire. Voluntary desire for anything but God and for the things God wants us to have is sin and idolatry. Evil thoughts soil our spirits. As our Master taught us: "First clean the inside of the cup and the plate, that the outside also may be clean." (Mt 23:28) "For from within, out of the heart of man, come evil thoughts, sexual immorality, theft, murder, adultery, coveting, wickedness, deceit, sensuality, envy, slander, pride, foolishness. All of these come from within and they defile a person." (Mk 7: 22-23, ESV) Therefore, the only way to rid our lives of sin is to root out evil thoughts that incline us to desire things other than God and His Kingdom.

The longer we entertain an evil thought, the more time the desire has to germinate in the soil of our hearts and increase its appeal to our free will. When we allow the evil attraction to remain, its power to arouse desire grows. Eve tarried with the evil thought and conversed with it as if it were a friend until it impregnated her and she brought forth its child, sin. Then sin brought death into the world. A green shoot is easily uprooted. Only with immense difficulty can a deeply rooted tree be torn out of the ground. We must uproot evil thoughts as soon as they arise.

An evil thought loses power over us when we reveal it in faith before God to another Christian. If we conceal an evil thought in our hearts, it grows in strength. Therefore, one of the main benefits of having a spiritual confidant in Christ (a mentor, guide, director, or friend) is disclosure and destruction of evil thoughts.

The Lord Jesus gave us the basic principle that guides all growth in Christian contemplation in these words: "Blessed are the pure of heart, for they shall see God." (Mt 5:3) We will be blessed with the vision of God to the extent that we discern and reject the evil attractions sown in our hearts before they become the voluntary desires that constitute sin. A mirror covered with mud, stains, and dirt will not give a clear reflection. The more our hearts are soiled by evil thoughts, the less clearly will we be able to see Jesus in the mirror of our spirits.

By prayer and spiritual discipline (as described later in this chapter), we can greatly reduce the quantity of evil thoughts that approach us. However, we cannot altogether prevent the approach of evil thoughts in this life. Until our Blessed Lord Jesus comes again, Christian life on earth will be a spiritual warfare, a lifelong struggle with the devil, the sower of evil thoughts. "For we do not wrestle against flesh and blood, but against the rulers, against the authorities, against the cosmic powers over this present darkness, against the spiritual forces of evil". (Eph 6:12)

FROM TEMPTATION TO SIN

Let us take note of how an evil thought moves from the phase of *attraction* (temptation) to the phase of voluntary *acceptance* (sin). God sows good seed in the field of our heart continuously and in abundance beyond measure. God does not want Satan's evil thoughts to approach us, but He uses them to purify us like gold. Evil thoughts are Satan's attempt to destroy us forever. God never allows the Evil One to tempt us beyond the strength of His grace within us. God always gives us the opportunity for escape from, or to gain the victory over, the evil thoughts He allows Satan to sow within us. What Satan intends for our destruction, God intends for our glorification. However, we have to make a choice. Either we take advantage of God's grace for victory over evil thoughts, or we ignore God's grace and freely enter into the temptation. Our *neglect of grace,* our failure to use the God-given means of victory or escape, is what allows an evil thought *merely sown as a conscious attraction* to become a deadly sin *fully grown voluntary acceptance.*

Once accepted, evil thoughts defile a person. They make us unfit to live in the presence of God and unfit to have God dwell within us. They disqualify a person for the true worship of God. As long as we fail to resist evil thoughts in our hearts, even our prayer becomes hypocrisy—like the Pharisee mentioned in of Luke's gospel (18:11) who gave a hypocrite's thanksgiving to God while he accepted the evil thought that he was "not like other people".

Here a word of caution is called for. God's love is not conditional upon the purity of our hearts. Do not confuse the loss of the vision of God caused by our evil thoughts with loss of God's unconditional love for all sinners. God's love is His freely given grace to us undeserving sinners. Our ability to see God's grace-love for us is what is diminished by our voluntarily accepted evil thoughts.

DISCERNMENT OF THOUGHTS: VIGILANCE

Described from the point of view of God's prior grace, discernment of thoughts is a divine gift that empowers the Christian to recognize whether a thought is from the Holy Spirit or from the Evil One. Described from the point of view of graced human action, discernment of thoughts is the practice of prayerful vigilance over the thoughts of the heart.

Evil thoughts are temptations insinuated by the Enemy. "Watch and pray that you may not enter into temptation," says the Lord (Mt 26:41). Peter similarly admonishes us: "Be sober, be *watchful*. Your adversary the devil prowls around like a roaring lion seeking someone to devour." (1 Pet 5:8).

If a person is not vigilant, not spiritually awake, she or he is spiritually asleep. This is not a sleep that restores our strength. It leads us to eternal death. To sleep the "sleep of death" means to be carelessly inattentive to the evil origin, nature, and effects of the thoughts that enter into our hearts. The "sleep of death" is the sin of willful moral unconsciousness. We sleep to what is wrong, while undiscerned evil thoughts carry us to eternal death. How rightly is this moral unconsciousness named the "sleep of death"! We can apply Our Lord's parable in Mt 13:25 to this morbid sleep. "At night, while men were sleeping", the "enemy" Satan, comes and sows weeds (evil thoughts) in the fields of our hearts. Therefore, in Ps 13: 3-4, we pray that God will give us the Light of Life (the Light is Jesus: Jn 12:12), that we may remain awake and vigilant, lest our Enemy have dominion over us:

> *Consider and answer me, O Lord my God;*
> *Give Light to my eyes, or I will sleep the sleep of death,*
> *and my Enemy will say: 'I have prevailed.'*

In the *sleep of death,* we shut our eyes to the Divine Light that awakens us to moral vigilance. Jesus is "the True Light Who enlightens all men" (Jn 1:9) When we close the eyes of our hearts to the Light of Christ, in this spiritual *sleep of death*, the light of conscience in us becomes darkness and how great is that darkness! (Cf. Mt 6:23)

TWO: PRACTICING DISCERNMENT

The Revealing Of The Thoughts

'An evil thought concealed grows in strength. An evil thought revealed looses its power.' This ancient wisdom expresses a basic principle of the utmost importance in the battle against evil thoughts. In view of this foundational truth, every Christian should have a personal spiritual confidant, a mature trustworthy Christian, with whom she or he meets regularly for the purpose of prayer and the revealing of the thoughts of the heart. Such a spiritual confidant is a true friend in Christ. At different places and times in Christian history, these friends have been called by various names: elder, pastor, priest, spiritual director, spiritual father or mother, mentor, guide, confessor, or simply a brother or sister in the Lord.

Do not confuse the sharing of private information that takes place in secular intimacy or psychotherapy with the revealing of thoughts that takes place in this sacred relationship. Uniquely in this case, two persons are consciously and intentionally gathered in the Name of Jesus. The two are united in a covenant of agape friendship, mutual prayer, and the reciprocal responsibility and transparency that is part of all true love. Jesus is in their midst.

He is there to defend, deliver, heal, and guide. More than the spiritual confidant, it is Jesus who receives the revealing of the thoughts. In this spiritual relationship, the one who confides and the confidant have faith in each other, but their trust is in Christ in their midst. Their meeting is an exercise of mutual love, prayer, and shared faith. Secular psychological counseling, although valid and valuable in its own right, cannot be described in these terms. We will reflect at length on this spiritual relationship in the next chapter as the Pathway of Spiritual Direction.

Method of Practicing Discernment

Our saintly ancestors in the faith, from the early centuries of the Christian era, have bequeathed to us the following method for struggling with demons, that is, for casting out evil thoughts sown by alien spirits. The practice of discernment is also known as "vigilance" and "guarding the heart". It is based on a simple imitation of what Jesus did when He was tempted by Satan's evil thoughts in the desert, and (2) a total reliance in prayer upon Jesus as our Savior. When an evil thought/spirit arises in your consciousness, conduct yourself as follows.

1. **Become aware of it.**

The power to become aware of the approach of an evil thought is offered to us as a gift of the Holy Spirit. It then becomes our responsibility to accept or to ignore this gift. We must *want* to wake up and become conscious of our inner life of thoughts and feelings. In order to become aware of our inner life, we will need to cultivate a certain amount of quiet, prayerful, and solitude in our lives. In the solitude of our own hearts, by inward attention, we can become competent in observing the thoughts that appear there.

In our natural condition, thoughts are our means for defending ourselves and for getting what we need to survive and thrive in the surrounding world of hostility and scarcity. After we first receive the revelation of divine love, we begin to learn to trust in God's protection and providence. By choosing to trust in the Love of God that has grasped us, we rely less upon our thoughts and plans to attain our goals. We think less the more we trust. Deepening faith increases the tranquility of our mind. Trust in divine love causes our racing thoughts slow down.

On the other hand, if we abandon ourselves to the tempo of the godless unbelieving world we will always be in turmoil, always trying to keep up with the human *race.* Never completely safe. Never having enough. Instead, we who have seen the Light must relax in the Light. We have Eternal Life. Nothing can separate us from the love God has for us in Christ Jesus. Our temporal and eternal well-being is as secure as God is true. Therefore, let us take possession of the peace Jesus gave us, living tranquilly in our hearts and from our hearts, where the victorious Jesus reigns serenely.

As we become less frantic, more centered and peaceful, we will become inwardly more sensitive to the flow of thoughts and affections in our hearts. By the inclination of our fallen nature, we do not want to perceive anything unflattering in our heart. We spontaneously try not to see what is wrong in our inner life of thought and feeling. Therefore, we need to ask God for the grace of humility to recognize the presence of evil thoughts.

We need not be afraid. He is infinitely compassionate. He knows of what we are made. God does not judge us for the wrong that He sees in us. His heart is to deliver us, not to condemn us. As long as we deny their existence, faithless loveless thoughts thrive within us. When we admit them and take them to Jesus, He cleanses us from them. The hypocrisy that Jesus deplored in the Pharisees was precisely their prideful refusal to become aware of the evil thoughts that were driving their murderous conduct.

The power to become aware of what is transpiring within our life of thought and feeling will increase as we learn to withdraw from the frantic rush of the secular world outside us and retreat to the quiet solitude of our inner self. There, the Light of Christ shines on the stream of our thoughts to make us aware.

2. **Name it.**

Our first awareness may be only a vague *general* impression that something is wrong with the thought, attitude, feeling, or mood we are experiencing. These undefined feelings of discomfort often arise from an interaction with another person that has gone sour, especially with persons who are emotionally close to us. We might ask ourselves: What need, want, or fear was I trying to take care of when the interaction went bad? We must look at the thought or feeling closely until we see it clearly enough to call it by name: fear of being (or thought to be) in the wrong, feeling criticized or judged, self-loathing, greed, pride, distrust of God, lust, or whatever it is. By naming it we drag it out of the obscurity in which it was hiding and expose it to the direct light of our conscience illumined by the Spirit.

3. **Contradict it.**

Because an evil thought is always a demonic lie, we must oppose it by a conscious affirmation of the divine truth that contradicts it. Use your own words, or better still, use a verse or thought from the Scriptures to contradict the evil thought. To illustrate: if you identify a feeling of guilt, as though your sins were not forgiven, contradict it *emphatically* with a statement of truth like: "There is no condemnation for those who are in Christ Jesus." (Rm. 8:1) Another example: if you feel anger toward one who wronged you, contradict the feeling by forgiving that person and praying for his or her salvation and happiness. One more illustration: If you become aware of any inordinate desire to have some material thing, remember and speak the opposing truth in words like: "Man shall not live by bread alone, but by every word that proceeds from the mouth of God". (Mt.4: 4) The general rule is: find the scriptural truth that contradicts the devil's lie and hurl it at the evil thought.

We often have to respond to evil thoughts or feelings towards us that arise in persons close to us. If you feel another person's hurt or anger arise in the course of an interaction, secretly ask yourself: What fear, hurt, or disappointment does this person feel that motivated their hurt or anger? Name it. In doubt, sensitively ask the other person to tell you what he or she is feeling and what caused it. Once you identify it, then engage the person with the truth that opposes the lie that has threatened or wounded the other. If he feels judged by what you said, contradict the feeling with words of personal affirmation. If the other thinks or feels you have spoken or acted in an unloving manner, express your sorrow and condemn the word or deed that was hurtful or perceived as hurtful. If you actually intended to say or do the evil word or deed then repent and ask forgiveness. If you did not intend it but it was misperceived as intentional, then gently explain your true intention. In every case, contradict the untrue thought with the truth.

In this spiritual exercise, we do not deny ours or others' unwanted evil thoughts and feelings. On the contrary, we first become fully aware of them and identify them by name. Then we make the choice to deny that these feelings or thoughts express the truth and love that we know by the revelation of Jesus Christ and want by His grace. We *choose* to love someone effectively by praying sincerely for him or her, in spite of feeling negatively toward the person. We *choose* to trust in God, in spite of our feelings of fear and uncertainty. We *choose* to entrust our life to our Father's Love when our emotions tell us He has abandoned us. In this "method of contradiction" we freely choose not to agree with the evil thought, and we contradict it by choosing to do the good thing that is the exact opposite of what the evil thought suggests.

4. **Annihilate it by Prayer**

After you have contradicted the lie, fix the attention of your heart and mind on Jesus Our Savior and ask Him to deliver you from the evil thought and from the spirit who sowed it. The very act by which you lift your attention to Jesus casts out, replaces, and annihilates the evil thought. The evil spirit is cast out along with his malign thought. As often as the thought returns, calmly and peacefully repeat this practice of annihilation of evil thoughts

Christians who practice some form of "unceasing prayer" such as the Jesus Prayer prevent the approach of innumerable evil thoughts. In a reciprocal fashion, women and men who are vigilant in discernment of the thoughts of their hearts gradually become people of incessant prayer because they are continually calling upon Jesus for deliverance.

By the practice of continually directing their attention to Jesus they annihilate evil thoughts already sown in the heart and they prevent the sowing of others.

The Divine Gift And The Human Practice Of Discernment

Every good deed of a Christian originates first as God's gift to us. When accepted, the gift becomes our life. Discernment is a gift of the Holy Spirit that becomes our life when we accept it. Discernment is *not* continuous reflective examination of the thoughts. It is the implicit vigilance of our love. Love in our heart is the judge of every thought that approaches. Through the sensitivity of love, the Spirit enables a person to recognize the approach of an evil thought (or spirit) even when she or he is not consciously practicing vigilance. Love never sleeps.

We see, therefore, that unceasing discernment is not a conscious activity. It is a subliminal concomitant function of our unceasing love. Yet, it is profitable to practice discernment reflectively at mid-day and at night before sleeping. We do this by pausing to reflect on how we have thought, felt, spoken, and acted during the day in relation to God, people, and in response to the events of the day. If we find anything in our thought, attitude, or conduct that expresses an unbelieving or unloving heart, we use the method of discernment as described above. If we realize that we have voluntarily *agreed* with some evil thought, we repent and turn to the Shed Blood of Jesus for forgiveness. Then we can abide in perfect peace knowing that Jesus has forgiven and delivered us from our sins.

I offer the following analogy to suggest how the gift of discernment works in us. The spiritual gift of continuous discernment may be compared to the natural sense of smell. Occasionally we consciously try to smell things, like perfume, flowers, or aromas of good food. Normally, however, we do not go around smelling everything! If we come close to something malodorous, such as rotten eggs, spoiled raw fish and the like, our sense of smell by itself will alert us. We do not have to think about it or *try* to smell bad things that come our way. So it is with the person who has the abiding gift of discernment. The spiritual stench of an approaching evil thought immediately calls the discernment-gifted Christian to attention.

The Lord within us watches over us. While we are busy doing His Will in our ordinary life, He guards us. At the moment an evil spirit puts a "seed thought" into our hearts, our Blessed Lord stirs us to moral awareness. This stirring of our souls by the Lord is the gift of discernment. We suddenly "smell" the evil of a demon-sown thought and we are aroused to discernment. Once we are put on conscious alert by the gift of discernment, it is our responsibility to put the gift into practice, using the method described earlier. If we disregard the gift of discernment, if we do not take heed to the "smell" of evil, then we *sleep in death*, that is, we surrender ourselves to the power of the devil. Unless we find repentance, this evil thought will lead us into sin, separation from God, the loss of love relationships, and eternal death. Therefore, be vigilant as the Lord commands: *"Watch and pray."*

Spiritual Discipline Of Mind And Heart

We have been considering discernment both as a habitual attitude and as a methodical practice for dealing with individual thoughts. However, if we increasingly fill our minds and hearts with the good things of the Spirit, we will close the door to the approach of innumerable of evil thoughts. Remember the teaching or our Blessed Lord Jesus (Mt 12: 43-45). He told us that once an evil spirit (thought) has been cast out, after wandering about seeking rest in waterless places, he comes back to person from whom he had been ejected. Even though he finds it swept and in order, if it is *empty*, he brings seven others worse than the first and they enter and dwell there. The key word here is "empty". By our baptismal faith, the evil spirit has been cast out. But we must not leave our personal spirit uninhabited.

There is no room for any evil thought or evil spirit to dwell in a heart already occupied by the Holy Spirit and filled with His thoughts of truth and love. Spiritual discipline of mind and heart means the effort we make to keep our inner spirit attentive to and filled with God and the thoughts of God.

As people think in their heart, so they are in their lives. (Cf. Mt.15: 18-20; Lk.6: 45) Therefore, St. Paul urges us to think good things: "...whatever is true, whatever is honorable, whatever is just, whatever is pure, whatever is lovely, whatever is gracious, if there is any excellence, if there is anything worthy of praise, *think about these things".* (Phil. 4:8)

It does not require a profound sociological analysis to observe that most of the mental and emotional activity of Americans is spent on things that have little or no eternal value…buying and selling, amassing wealth, material security, health, the national political conversation, sports and entertainment, the quest for beauty, romance, sex, and pleasure. If we are not going to be conformed to this age, we have to carry out a twofold spiritual discipline of mind and heart:

(1) *Withdrawal of your mind and heart from the sinful, or merely useless, concerns, values, and interests and activities of the unbelieving world.* In practice, this means reducing our participation in the goals, activities, and conversation of the world that is oblivious of God. Concretely: Turn off the media more! Limit the amount of your recreational pastimes. After a certain point, these engagements go beyond restorative recreation and become a waste of life. Unless you are ministering to the lost, avoid at least some of your unnecessary conversation with people who do not care much about Jesus and His concerns. Instead, silently converse with God in your heart about life, love, scripture and all your hopes. Practice some prayerful silence of the tongue and of the mind. Secretly breathe the Name upon persons with whom you cannot speak of Jesus.

(2) *Immersion of your mind and heart in the thoughts and things of God.* These holy thoughts from God are available to us in the sacred scriptures and in the sacrament of the Lord's Supper. We think the thoughts of God in regular bible studies whether

Pathways to Union with Jesus

alone or with others, in holy conversations with other Christians about the things of God; in serving the poor, being kind and compassionate to all, in carefully fulfilling our familial and professional responsibilities, in faithful Sunday worship in our church, in being loyal in friendship, constant in prayer, reading the writings of the saints of old and of today, in communing with God in nature, and in worthy human art and music, and in bearing our suffering patiently as a blessed sharing in the sufferings of Jesus.

If we choose to surround ourselves with nominal Christians who are lukewarm in their pursuit of holiness, we will be lukewarm followers of Christ. It is not enough to practice the spiritual disciplines in solitude. We are sent into the world by Christ to form a community of friends in Christ and to belong to a community of worship alive in the Holy Spirit. A person can fulfill his or her mission in life and grow in personal holiness only in a life of faith shared with other Christians who are earnestly pressing on to the goal of the upward call of God in Christ Jesus. Christian life *is* community life. Without sharing the mind of Christ with a community of faith protects and confirms our personal discernment.

THREE: DISCERNING THE PERSONAL GIFTS OF GOD

Gifts Of Ministry

With regard to gifts of ministry, the rule for discernment is simple: Listen to the church. Ministry gifts are powers to serve the community of faith given by the Spirit to the individual to build up the church. These gifts will be recognized and encouraged by the church. The church will tell you if you have the gift of teaching, or song, or administration, or liturgical leadership, or spiritual counseling, or healing prayer, etc. There is no need to trumpet your gifts of ministry. The gifts the Spirit gives speak for themselves. Even if –as sometimes happens— the church fails to recognize and utilize your gifts of ministry, do not become resentful. Accept the humiliation. So doing you will advance in likeness to Christ, whose gifts of ministry the leaders of His people did not recognize. God will open other doors of ministry for you when your church group fails to receive your gifts.

Gifts Of Good Deeds

All of our good deeds in word and work are personal gifts of God. These gifts are the *particular will* of God for a person at any given moment. God's gift to a person is His *preference* for that person at that time. Every good thought, word, or deed that we choose moment by moment is God's gracious gift to us. These personal gifts are not absolute commandments; they are God's loving invitations that reveal His preferences for us.

The *general will* of God is easy to discern because it is absolute and definite: do evil to no one and love your neighbor as yourself. When we feel an inclination to act contrary to God's general will it is not difficult to identify the impulse as an evil thought. It is a clear choice between manifest objective good and evil.

Discerning the *particular will* of God for us, His preference, is far more subtle. Here we have to decide between good alternatives. The vast majority of our daily words and deeds are manifestations of God's *preferential will*, His particular gift to us in the moment. These particular gifts present themselves continually everyday, mostly concerning matters of lesser importance, like: "Shall I pray now or read scripture?" However, sometimes our preferential personal choices in the moment have the power to change the rest of our lives forever: "Shall I return a phone call to the attractive woman I casually met at the coffee shop?" How vastly important it is for us to discern these life-determining impulses rightly!

To discern the general will of God we need only to consult our conscience illumined by faith. To discern the particular will of God, His preference for us in the moment, we have to recognize the voice of God speaking in our hearts. Our power to discern the preferential will of God will be as strong as our heart is pure and our love is deep. The devotional pathways you are studying in this book lead progressively to purity of heart and to love. A Christian of pure heart has a connatural spiritual sensitivity that 'knows' the subtle preferential will of God, *without knowing how she knows.*

We know that what God prefers is always what He knows is best for us. However, God's preferences are not commandments. It is not a sin if we do not follow God's preferences. A divine invitation is not a demand. God's proffered gift is not an obligation. We are completely free in these matters of divine preference. Nevertheless, following our own will instead of God's preference prevents us from receiving the best gifts God wants us to have; or worse, choosing our own preference may bring upon us some painful suffering God would rather have spared us. God has shown in scripture that He is always willing to love us by yielding to our preferences even when we choose not to embrace His. When we do not receive the gift of God's preferential will, we make our lives harder, but He will always be with us. He will even use the selfish choices we make instead of choosing His preferential will, to realize His "plan B" for our spiritual growth and glory…but doing it "our way" will entail more suffering.

When we ask: "What is God's particular will for me at this moment of my life?" we are really asking, "What gift of life has God prepared from all eternity for me to walk in right now?" (Cf. Eph. 2:11) What I am to do today or tomorrow has been in the mind of God forever. Our present deeds are God's eternal thoughts. Now, "who knows a person's thoughts except the spirit of that person which is in him? So also, no one comprehends the thoughts of God except the Spirit of God. Now we have received not the spirit of the world, but the Spirit which is from God, *that we might understand the gifts bestowed on us by God.*" (1Cor 2:11-12) What we are to do now is God's gift bestowed upon us in the present moment. We can know it!

Living In God's Will: The Unknowing Of Freedom

When we do the will of God expressed in law and in our moral conscience, we enjoy the intellectual certainty of knowing we are doing God's will. There is very great comfort in knowing with rational certainty that we are acting according to the will of God. However, intellectual certainty is not available to us when we do God's preferential will. We make our choice to do God's preferential will, not on purely rational grounds but by 'the inclination of our heart'. Living by choice is a fearful thing. But we can trust God to guide our choice if we are surrendered to Him in love. We may then safely follow the bold declaration of St. Augustine: "Love, and do what you want".

If we humbly pray for divine guidance, God will answer our earnest prayer: "Incline my heart O Lord to thy testimonies." (Ps. 119:3) After we pray, listen to counsel, and wait on the Lord to incline our hearts, we finally make our choice, daring to believe that the inclination of our own heart manifests God's preferential will for us. Do not to confuse this spiritual discernment with the sensualist principle of pop culture morality: "If it feels good, do it." The spiritual gift of discernment is an act of prevailing free will, not an act of prevailing feeling. In following a God-given 'inclination of our heart' to do God's preferential will, we make a conscientious decision, even if it is contrary to our emotional preference.

The Spirit pours love into our hearts. Love gives us a spiritual intuition of God's preference for our lives, beyond the reach of our reason and emotion. The intuition of love reveals God's preferential gifts to us in the moment. "What no eye has seen, nor ear heard nor the heart of man imagined, what God has prepared for those who love him. These things God has revealed to us through the Spirit." (1 Cor 2:9)

TO THE PATHWAY OF SPIRITUAL DIRECTION

Communal Discernment Of Thoughts: Spiritual Direction

We practice Lectio Divina, the Jesus Prayer, and Discernment of Thoughts, in the solitude of our own inner spirit. In the practice of Spiritual Direction, we share our inner spiritual life with the church in the person of our confidant. The meeting for spiritual direction forms the nuclear church where two are gathered in His Name.

The Lord Jesus comes to the two Christians who gather in His Name for spiritual direction. As He did with Cleopas and his friend on the evening of the Resurrection, Jesus joins the two spiritual companions on their spiritual journey. With us as with them, in the fellowship of spiritual direction, Jesus purifies our hearts from false impressions and replaces them with the truth of God. The two, walking together with Jesus, are inspired with burning hearts for their mission in the life that lay before them.

When we study the earliest records of spiritual direction, which we find in the Sayings of the Desert Fathers (Fourth Century), we learn that spiritual direction took place in the context of a visit between friends in the Spirit. The "visitor" was typically—but not always—a younger Christian who held the elder, more experienced, Christian, in high esteem. The elder responded in love by receiving the visitor with warm hospitality. The visitor was motivated by a desire to reveal the thoughts and questions of his heart to a wise, loving, prayerful, and trusted senior. The younger made the visit in the hope that God would use the words and prayers of the elder to purify and enlighten his heart and mind. The elder's blessing was a confirmation to the visitor that he was living and advancing in the Spirit of Christ toward greater maturity in agape-love.

Christian wisdom from ages past tells us: *An evil thought concealed grows in power, but an evil thought revealed in humility before God to a brother or sister loses power and finally is cast out.* On the other hand, the good thoughts, actions, and experiences God gives us are protected, confirmed, and enhanced by the affirmation of a mature spiritual companion. A person leaves the spiritual direction visit with a blessed sense of being confirmed in his or her life of faith.

In the following chapter, we will study Spiritual Direction as a Pathway to union with Jesus.

CHAPTER FIVE

THE PATHWAY OF SPIRITUAL DIRECTION

SPIRITUAL DIRECTION

INTRODUCTION

The Scriptures give us advice and examples that indicate that we should have a companion in the spiritual life whom we trust completely and to whom we open our hearts.

> "Two are better than one, because they have a good reward for their toil. For if they fall, one will lift up his fellow. But woe to him who is alone when he falls
> and has not another to lift him up.
> Again if two lie together, they are warm; but how can one be warm alone?
> And though a man might prevail against one who is alone,
> two will withstand him.
> A threefold cord is not quickly broken."(Ecc. 4:9-12)

When the Lord sent His apostles out on mission, He sent them in pairs (Mk 11: 2; 14:13). When He appointed seventy others, he "sent them on ahead of Him, *two by two* into every town and place where He Himself was about to come." (Lk 10:1)

Jesus brings two people together and empowers them to accomplish a work of the Spirit that they would not be able to do alone. Where two are gathered in the Name, a Third is present, Jesus. The text from Ecclesiastes quoted above, speaks about the strength of two men, but ends in verse 12 by saying "a *threefold* cord is not easily broken". Two persons united in the Name of Jesus to do the work of the Spirit are wound together around the Third Cord: Jesus Christ Almighty. Who can break it!

This "two" that becomes "three", where the Third is Jesus, takes place in all friendships in Christ, and in a supreme way in the sacramental friendship of marriage. Spiritual direction is another unique expression of Christian friendship. Christ makes Himself present to the two who walk together in the spiritual journey and converse about Jesus in their lives. Cleopas and his friend had a shared experience of Jesus in their midst as they talked about their religious experience on their journey together. So it is with two who gather for spiritual direction.

I am writing out this theoretical and practical instruction on Spiritual Direction as a pathway to union with Jesus in order to enable and encourage the reader to reap the rich spiritual benefits of this tradition of Christian spirituality. The conceptual model of spiritual direction presented here, and the details of practice, do not represent the only correct form. There are many other valid ways to engage in spiritual direction. I believe this ancient model will serve you well, but choose the form of spiritual direction that works best for you.

The Tradition Of The Spiritual Father/Mother

From the writings of the Desert Fathers, we learn of the historical beginnings of this specific practice of spiritual friendship that we now call "spiritual direction". The phrase "spiritual direction" would have been unintelligible to the saints of the third and fourth centuries. They thought in terms of a spiritual parent and child relationship. However, unlike the natural family relationship, in spiritual direction there is no natural structure of authority and obedience. The spiritual parent and child are equals before God and in mutual esteem.

Both the name and form of spiritual direction have varied over the centuries. Beneath the many variations, we can identify the following essential elements of the tradition. Two Christians meet with the conscious intention of being in the presence of Christ. They agree to dedicate the meeting to prayerful attention to the spiritual life of one of them.

Pathways to Union with Jesus

The Christian who initiates the relationship intends to open her heart, by revealing her inner thoughts, both dark and light. The younger seeker submits her moral and spiritual experience to the care, prayer, judgment, comment, and encouragement of the spiritual "elder". She also seeks from the elder 'a word of life', that is, some thought inspired by the Spirit, to guide her life. The person serving as elder gives loving attention, care, prayer, and whatever word of wisdom God provides.

Christian history has left us different names for the participants in the relationship of spiritual direction. Jesus was called "Master" and those He guided spiritually were called His "disciples". St Paul spoke of his younger disciple, Timothy, as a "son with a father". (Phil 2: 22) In the relationship of personal spiritual guidance in early monasticism, the leader was called an "abba" (father) or "amma" (mother). Medieval monasticism referred to an "abbot" or "abbess" as the spiritual guides of the "brothers" or "sisters" of the monastery. In the later Roman Catholic Church, "confessor and penitent" became common designators. Recent centuries gave us the rather pretentious title, "spiritual director". In common use today are names like "mentor", "accountability partner", "fellowship brother", "elder", "pastor", or "spiritual companion or friend". Where there is faith and sincerity in all these forms, the Holy Spirit is certain to be present and active.

The form presented here comes from the practice and writings of monks of the Fourth Century, modified to fit the circumstances of contemporary Christian society. For the ancients, spiritual direction took the form of a specific kind of *visit between friends in the Spirit.* Therefore, we will name the person who receives direction the *visitor,* or *visiting friend, guest, younger, seeker, or directee.* The person who gives the spiritual direction we will refer to as the *host*, or *hosting friend, elder, or director*.

The Paradigm Of Spiritual Direction: A Visit Between Friends

One of the influences of modern psychology upon Christian spirituality has been to lead our contemporaries to think of spiritual direction in the terms of a clinical psychotherapeutic model. An office, like that of a psychological counselor or therapist, is commonly thought to be the appropriate setting for spiritual direction. The spiritual director is often seen as a professional with specialized training, again like a therapist or teacher, who can be expected to help her or his "client" or "student" because of superior learning, professional training, or personal excellence in the field of spirituality.

There are some superficial similarities between spiritual direction and psychotherapy but they are worlds apart in substance. The Holy Spirit is the Principal Agent in spiritual direction. The goal is transformation of heart and mind into the likeness of Christ. The relationship is between equals in Christ. Spiritual direction is an act of faith on the part of both participants. Does any of this resemble psychotherapy?

In the fourth century Christian monastic literature the "visitor" was typically a younger Christian who held the older or more experienced Christian in high esteem. The "elder" welcomed the visitor with warm hospitality but did not consider himself in any way superior to the younger. The visitor came to reveal his temptations and troubling thoughts to the elder. He believed God would use the words and prayers of the elder to help him avoid the pitfalls of evil thoughts and strengthen his resolve to seek God.

The seeker in ancient times would go to the dwelling (that is, the hermitage) of the elder and knock on the door. The elder received the visitor with physical and spiritual hospitality. A later Father of Monasticism, St Benedict, captured the spirit of the host by saying that the visitor should be received as Christ. In our day, spiritual companions often find it convenient to meet each other at church, at home, in their places of work, or even at a restaurant or coffee shop. Having something to eat or drink together was a regular part of the "spiritual direction session" in the desert.

The difference between a spiritual direction visit and any other social visit is the conscious and explicit intention of the participants: they meet to honor God and to seek spiritual growth. With this specific goal in mind, the two do not spend too much time in small talk. After some opening pleasantries about their lives in general, they narrow the focus to the spiritual life of the visitor.

In this model, spiritual direction is a sacramental relationship between two Christians, as friends and equals, who are seeking spiritual growth together in their relationship. Friends are equals even though, as Christians, they hold each other in higher esteem. This equality and mutual esteem remains in tact even though the visit is structured by specific devotional roles. The receiving Christian carries out the role of the host and the other carries out the role of the visitor. The visitor (seeker) implicitly or explicitly

Pathways to Union with Jesus

asks the host (director) to accompany him or her with loving discernment and prayer on the spiritual journey. The host obediently gives this companionship. The director/host does not trust her own or his own power or wisdom, however, but prayerfully relies entirely upon God to act in the spiritual life of the visitor.

The host considers herself or himself a privileged companion but not the "director" of the spiritual life of the visitor. The host knows that the Holy Spirit is the only true Spiritual Director. The roles of the host and visitor are established, controlled, maintained, and evaluated chiefly on *the authority and initiative of the visitor*. The visitor confers authority in the relationship upon the host. The host does not pretend to have any personal authority or superior wisdom.

The host does not assume a position of "superior" in the relationship, but rather one of "obedient servant". The spiritual director trusts in God to give the guidance, grace, and wisdom to the visitor by means of the relationship. The host considers her or his role to be that of a conduit, not a source —God being the only Source of every grace.

At no time does the visiting friend relinquish to the host his or her own responsible judgment. When the visitor accepts the thought and guidance offered by the host it is because it seems right in his of her own best judgment. The visitor does not submit blindly to the ideas or directives of the host. Spiritual direction begins with the moral independence of the visiting friend and pursues the goal of rendering the visitor completely submitted to, inspired, and guided by the Spirit of God.

The practice of spiritual direction cooperates with God's grace for the *transformation of consciousness* of the visitor. This transformation gradually brings the practitioner to think about God, himself, other persons, and the whole cosmos in the light of revelation. In other words, spiritual direction is a means of grace that works to bring the practitioner to know and love all things as God knows and loves them. This is the unceasing prayer of the spiritual director for the visitor who comes to him.

Spiritual direction also brings about a *transformation of the heart.* Its goal is to foster in the visitor an increasingly full reception of the divine gift of perfect love, agape. No one expects the complete attainment of this in this mortal life, but the exhilarating excitement of the spiritual life lies in the forward progress that is always available at every moment until the last heartbeat! The spiritual seeker in Christ lives in the conviction that "more and better" is always immediately ahead and attainable in this life. The host desires and prays for unceasing growth of love in the heart of the visiting friend even as he prays for his own soul.

The Immediate Goal Of Spiritual Direction: Discernment

The grace of God is the original source and efficient cause of progress toward the ultimate moral goal of Christian life: perfect love. Discernment enables a Christian to choose deeds that express love in the world. God's grace provides both the seed and the growth of discernment of thoughts. The host and the visitor agree from the outset, consciously, intentionally, and prayerfully, to seek the gift of discernment of thoughts for the visitor *as the immediate goal* of their relationship in spiritual direction.

Discernment is a gift of the Holy Spirit to believers. This gift enables us to distinguish between what is true or false and what agrees with or contradicts the revelation of Divine love as revealed in Jesus Christ. This gracious "judgment of the heart" can be exact even when the mind is unable to reach rational certainty. Scripture refers to this experience as "walking in the spirit", that is, living and acting by the impulse of the Spirit. In the sharing that takes place in spiritual direction, the visitor's discernment is enhanced, strengthened, recognized, and confirmed —or it is sharpened by being called into question by the silent or spoken discernment of the host. A mature loving host prays continually for the increase of the gift of discernment for his or her visiting friend.

The Ultimate Goal Of Spiritual Direction: To Be Filled And Led By The Spirit

The final goal of spiritual direction is identical with the goal of a person's whole life in Christ: to be a bearer of the Spirit of God (pneumatophor) and to be borne by the Spirit of God (pneumatikos). Instead of the unruly impulses of the natural psyche, the mature Christian increasingly recognizes and yields to the impulses of the Indwelling Holy Spirit. Filled by the Spirit, the Christian is also led by the Spirit. In ideal perfection, never fully attained in this mortal life, a follower of Jesus would *always* think, feel, choose, act, and respond *as inspired by the Divine Indwelling Spirit*. She would live, no longer her natural self, but only and always Christ would live in her.

The host and visitor agree in prayer to pursue the ideal of spiritual perfection, namely, that the visitor be led by the Holy Spirit, always, exclusively, and completely. Not even the great Saint Paul fully attained this perfection. Like him, however, we must keep on striving for it, until the Holy Spirit becomes the only law, written on our hearts, governing all of our being and action (Phil.3: 12-14).

In his conscious moral life, a mature Christian strives to place himself freely and fully under the power of the Holy Spirit. As he progresses in spiritual discernment the advancing Christian is increasingly able to know what is the perfect will of God in every circumstance and at each instant of his life. Although open and receptive to every human influence, he no longer lives by submission to the guidance of anyone outside himself. In, and under, the power and authority of the Indwelling Spirit, he becomes more autonomous. He judges all things and himself is judged by no one. (1Cor 2:15) Caution: Let us who are not yet mature not attempt this spiritual autonomy prematurely before the time.

Spiritual autonomy is a distinctive moral quality of a person who is inspired by the Indwelling Spirit. Increasing autonomy in the Spirit is, therefore, pursued and expected as the end result of spiritual direction. A mature Christian obeys the counsels of her chosen spiritual elder and the statutes of State and Church because the judgment of his spiritual discernment tells him it is the will of God to do so. The Holy Spirit guides the conscience and discernment of the Christian who is surrendered to Him. There is no higher authority than this.

As a young monk, I was educated to obey church authorities as if they were vicars of Christ. (Which they are, I still believe, but only in so far as they command what God commands.) The ecclesiastical superiors frequently held up to us "subjects", as an example to be imitated, the prompt obedience of blessed John the Calligrapher. John was an Egyptian monk and a copyist of the fourth or fifth century. One day his abbot asked him to go on an errand. John immediately stopped working and ran to do the will of the "superior". The abbot looked at the manuscript John had been working on and noticed that the monk was so prompt in his obedience that had not paused even long enough to cross the Greek letter tau, "T", he was writing.

Years later, when I was studying the primary texts of the desert fathers, I found another story about the same blessed John the Calligrapher. My church authorities never mentioned this one. You will see why it was suppressed when I recount it to you. The same abbot as in the previous story commanded

Pathways to Union with Jesus

blessed John to do something that John thought was contrary to the demands of monastic renunciation of the world. John obeyed, but with inner conflict. Then he told his ecclesiastical superior: 'Father, I pray thee not to command me again to act contrary to my conscience, lest I be forced to disobey thee'. John had attained *autonomy in the Spirit.* A Christian's conscience, that is, his best spiritual discernment, may not always be objectively correct in its judgment, but it must always be obeyed.

There are times in every Christian's life when she or he knows that they cannot trust their own judgment in some matter. In these instances, it is true wisdom and spiritual discernment to choose to think and act according to the judgment of a trusted Christian friend or elder. However, there is nothing "blind" about this obedience. This Christian has the grace of discernment to know that he cannot trust his own judgment in the matter at hand. She makes the spiritual discernment, the decision of conscience, that she can trust the judgment of the other friend or elder in Christ. To know when you do not know is a very great gift of knowledge!

The Sacrament Of Spiritual Direction

The relationship we have with our spiritual director is a continuation of our relationship with Jesus. It embodies our interior, invisible, relationship with God and makes it visibly present in the outer world of space and time. Spiritual direction is a form of Christian friendship that expresses our free, independent, and spontaneous submission to our one and only Master, Father, and Teacher. (Cf. Mt. 23:9)

A sacrament may be described as "a visible sign of invisible grace", or, "a human relationship within which our spiritual relationship with God is actualized and made present in the material world". Spiritual direction, that is, the relationship between a Christian visitor and a spiritual friend as host, is a sacramental relationship. The elements of bread and wine that we share in the sacrament of Holy Communion are not, in themselves, the Lord and Savior, Jesus Christ. He fills the lowly elements with the fullness of His Glorious Presence. Analogously, the spiritual director is not the Blessed Lord either, but the Lord comes into the midst of the two who are gathered in His Name. He answers their faith that He will guide the thoughts and words of the visitor and the host. He fills their lowly human encounter with His Divine Presence and makes it a divine encounter. The host and the visitor do not receive merely each other. They receive Jesus in each other.

Spiritual Direction: Equal Persons In Complementary Roles

Friendship presupposes equality between the friends. If two persons are unequal before being united in friendship, the friendship itself makes them equals. Either the prince renounces his throne or his beloved commoner becomes a princess. Jesus, the Incarnate Word, renounced His divinity in time so that His Beloved commoner might share His divinity in eternity. As a form of Christian friendship, spiritual direction must be a relationship between equals. Friends visit each other. When one visits, the other plays the role of host. One friend serves as host and the other friend is served as guest, without there being any relationship of inferior to superior. It is the same in the visit between a Christian and his or her spiritual director: equal friends carry out complementary roles. One makes the gift of a visit. The other responds with the gift of hospitality.

Friends *agree* with each other; they do not do *dominate* or *submit* to each other. It follows, therefore, that the relationship between the two persons in spiritual direction is made perfect in *agreement,* not in *submission*. *Agreement in the Spirit* is the objective in spiritual direction just as it is between the members of the entire community of faith. (Mt 18:19; I Cor 1:10; 2 Cor 13:11) During our journey through life in the Spirit of Christ, we seek to enter into and to develop spiritual relationships of mutual agreement. To the extent that we live in the "flesh", we divide into hierarchies of superiors and subjects and we engage in relationships of domination and submission.

The Foundation Of Spiritual Direction In Faith.

Faith means, in the first place, our self-surrendering acceptance of Jesus Christ as Son of God and Savior of the World. By extension, faith means every additional act of faith by which we recognize a manifestation of God's will or Spirit in our lives. The first meaning of faith is objective and common to all believers. The second meaning is subjective and particular to each person. God reaches us, and He is reached by us, through both objective and subjective faith. Christians believe that every detail of their lives is a manifestation of God's love for them. Their subjective personal faith flows out of the objective faith common to all believers.

In spiritual direction both persons choose to believe that the relationship is a gift of God. The subjective devotional faith of the Christian seeking direction is the original foundation for beginning and maintaining a spiritual direction relationship. The host/director enters into this faith. Both believe God will use the relationship explicitly for the visitor's spiritual growth and implicitly for the growth of the host.

The Christian seeker does not place himself simply under a human spiritual director. He places himself under the Holy Spirit, whom he discerns to be acting in the love and wisdom of the director. He submits to and obeys the Spirit of God *always* and *unconditionally*. He submits to and obeys the spiritual director to the extent that he believes the host is enlightened and inspired by the Divine Spirit. Even a good spiritual director can have a blind spot. If a visiting Christian cannot have faith that the host is being led by the Spirit in a particular matter, he must quietly insulate himself from the influence of the director regarding that matter.

The *faith of the visitor*, more than the gifts or excellence of the hosting spiritual director, enables God's grace to flow into the relationship. To illustrate this point, I will paraphrase a story I remember from my early years of study of the Desert Fathers.

Pathways to Union with Jesus

In the fourth century, in the monastic desert of Egypt, it came to pass that one of the solitary monks fell away from his promise. His love and devotion grew cold. Life as a celibate monk became unendurably boring. In his human weakness, he took a woman into his dwelling, though secretly. The illicit couple even begot two children. Because he lived in a very remote part of the desert, it was possible to keep this secret for a long time. Until…

Back in Alexandria, a boy in his late teens was visited by the Holy Spirit with a passion for God. The young man was on fire for "God Alone". He wanted to dedicate his whole life to seeking union with God. To this end, he went out into the desert to live the rest of his life in prayer, innocence, and renunciation of the world, the flesh, and the devil. He first went looking for an older monk whom he would ask to become his teacher and guide. As Providence would have it, he came upon the abode of the fallen monk.

When the young man knocked, the demoralized old monk refused to answer the door. Instead, he shouted through the closed door telling the young fellow to go away. The last thing he wanted was a "disciple"! He expected the lad to be discouraged and leave. But he didn't. Undaunted during three days of knocking at the door and patiently waiting

Pathways to Union with Jesus

outside, the young Christian bolstered his hope by saying to himself: "This holy old man is testing me, to see if I will persevere in knocking. That is how the great Saint Anthony treated Blessed Paul when he came to become a disciple."

Exasperated, the old monk finally decided to disillusion the young man and get rid of him. He opened the door and invited the young seeker to come in. He flat out told the boy that he could not be his spiritual father because he was an unfaithful monk. And to make the point even more strongly, he called to a back room and the woman came out with the two little children clinging at her side. "Behold the fruit of my sin!" he blurted out to the wide-eyed young man. At this, the young man, without skipping a breath, charged back: "Then as you shall be my spiritual father, so shall your wife be my spiritual mother and your children shall be my brother and sister in Christ Jesus." All of them were overcome with emotion. The young man's word of faith proved to be prophetic. For they lived together just as he said and they all grew to full stature in Christ Jesus.

We see in this ancient story how the "younger" Christian, who was more advanced in the Spirit, became the disciple of an "elder" who was spiritually behind him. Note how they were all blessed, not in proportion to the excellence of the elder but according to the measure of the faith of the one who came to visit seeking direction *from God* through the elder.

Do not create false superiors. The greatness, sanctity, wisdom, or charismatic power, of a spiritual director is not the source of growth in a relationship of spiritual direction. The *faith* of the sincere seeker enables the relationship to become fruitful under God's grace. God responds to the *faith* of the Christian by using the hosting friend and the relationship for the spiritual good of both.

The Subject Matter Of Spiritual Direction

The subject matter of spiritual direction is the conscious, intentional, spiritual life of the Christian. Regrettably, many Christians have neither a reflective awareness of their spiritual life nor a conscious intention to cultivate it. One of the traditional methods Christian seekers use to become consciously intentional about their spiritual life is to compose and follow a personal rule of life.

Personal Rule Of Life

Either implicitly and non-reflectively, or consciously and intentionally, everyone has a personal "rule of life". Each person has in her heart some kind of "criteria for moral activity". We would not be human if we did not have a code of conduct that we expect of ourselves and by which we evaluate our activity. It might be as mechanical and tyrannical as the Freudian "super-ego" or it may be as free and gentle as the whisper of the Spirit's impulse. To have some kind of mental "rule of life" is as intrinsic to being human as it is to have a conscience. If we do not consciously and reflectively compose our rule of life, our conduct and conscience are liable to be guided by instincts, taboos, psychological mechanisms, soul wounds, unexamined assumptions, and social prejudices. By composing a personal rule of life we gain a conscious, intelligent, faith-enlightened, freely chosen set of moral goals, limits, and values.

Whether explicitly written or written only on the heart, the spiritual life that a Christian brings to a spiritual director is enshrined in her or his rule of life. The Christian opens her heart to the spiritual director. She confesses her failures, shares her victories, confides her hopes, and brings forth her innermost thoughts, good and evil. In revealing her heart, she reveals her personal rule of life.

Most Christians live by an unwritten rule of life. If the Spirit prevails in our lives, we do not need any written rule. Nevertheless, if you have never written down your personal rule of life, you may find a great blessing in doing so. It will help you know yourself and your agenda in life in a clearer light.

A rule of life is easy to compose. Prayerfully reflect on your relationship with God in Christ and your relationships with the people God has placed in your life. Write down what you believe would be the most complete fulfillment of each of these relationships. Then write down the concrete actions you are going to take in order to reach these goals. Write down your stronger personal gifts of service. Then write down the ways in which you are able to use your gifts for others. Your writing will identify your mission in your life in the world and the best way you know how to accomplish it. Any written rule is imperfect but it is a starting point. Keep in mind that future events and circumstances will reveal new dimensions of your mission in the world from Christ. You will modify and improve your rule as you learn from your experience and from the Spirit on your journey through life. Ask your spiritual director what she or he thinks of your rule. He or she will confirm your personal rule of life or perhaps help you improve it

The Form Of Spiritual Direction

We will describe the formal elements of the practice of spiritual direction in three parts: (1) The Meeting, (2) The Role of the Visitor (3) The Role of the Host.

(1) The Meeting

Both participants should prepare for the meeting by praying for each other. Prior to the meeting, the Christian should mentally (or on paper) note the important thoughts and experiences he or she ought to reveal to the hosting friend. The host should pray to become a better, more perceptive listener, both to the visitor, and to what the Holy Spirit would have him say to the visiting friend.

The frequency and duration of meetings for spiritual direction are determined by the amount required for the optimum benefit of the visiting friend. The amount will vary depending on the spiritual maturity of the visitor and on the diversity of events and circumstances in his life. Normally, a spiritual direction visit takes about 30 to 60 minutes, and the frequency of meetings range from once a week to once a month.

What about meeting by electronic media? Face-to-face meetings are always preferable. However, experience has demonstrated that once a good relationship has been established in person, precious elements of spiritual direction can take place through a meeting by phone, email, etc. when a person-to-person meeting is physically impossible. The same must be said of written communication.

A sudden deep sorrow, a moral fall, an extraordinary spiritual experience, an acute crisis or temptation, and other reasons sometimes move a Christian to visit the host friend apart from the appointed meeting. The host friend should give the visiting friend a warm invitation to come for a visit, apart from regularly scheduled meetings, whenever something extraordinary happens in the visitor's inner or outer world.

The Holy Conversation

At the meeting, after initial greetings and prayer, the holy conversation begins. The two people may be related in other ways, such as colleagues at work, church members, etc. It is natural to have some preliminary conversation about shared interests. It is important, however, not to spend too much time in general conversation before moving to the subject matter of spiritual direction.

Christian spirituality as a whole leads to a transformation of consciousness. The old ego-consciousness inherited from Adam must decrease. It is gradually replaced with "the mind of Christ". The practice of spiritual direction helps us grow in the new consciousness. The host presents herself as a willing and loving listener, silently inviting the other Christian to tell her thoughts. The visitor reads from the screen of his own mind telling the host about the person he is seeking to become in Christ, what are his final goals and immediate objectives, and what he is finding helpful or hurtful along the path. The holy conversation provides the visiting friend with a God-given opportunity to articulate and become more aware of who he is and what he wants in his Christian life. The listening host and the self-disclosing visitor are united in one sole intention: that the visiting friend may recognize the gifts of God in his life, while searching out and destroying any "thought" that impedes his ability to receive them. The host serves as a loving, mirror-like, consciousness in which the visitor can see and know his new self in Christ with increasing clarity.

After the holy conversation is complete, a prayer by either or both persons ends the meeting. One single meeting is a complete grace in itself. A series of meetings for spiritual direction is common practice but it is not absolutely necessary. However, if they both implicitly believe that another visit or visits seems desirable, the visitor (not the host) should take the initiative to suggest setting a date and time for the next meeting.

(2)   The Role Of The Visitor

To Be Consistent In Faith In The Host

The Christian visitor confers leadership in spiritual direction upon the sister or brother from whom she asks this service. He or she then has the self-imposed responsibility in faith to receive the word of that director as a sacrament of God's word to her. The visitor withholds agreement with the director only when she finds the word of the host to be in conflict with the written word of God, or otherwise in contradiction to her faith and morals.

To Reveal The Thoughts Of The Heart

The revealing of an evil thought to a fellow Christian, in the presence of God, destroys the power of that thought over our life, but revealing a Spirit-sown thought strengthens it. Revelation of the thoughts is of the very essence of spiritual direction. Those who cannot or will not reveal their innermost thoughts, humiliating as they may be, cannot profit from spiritual direction. Protection and deliverance from evil thoughts is undoubtedly one of the greatest benefits of having a spiritual director. The Christian who is willing to humble himself or herself by this confession will be saved from untold harm and inherit inestimable spiritual blessings.

Selection Of Matters To Be Revealed In Spiritual Direction

Between meetings, the Christian is trying to be responsible to: (1) his rule of life –at least in the unwritten form of his conscience, (2) the personal relationships God has entrusted to him, (3) the use of her spiritual gifts, special inspirations and leadings of the Holy Spirit. A Christian can report to his spiritual elder on any of these aspects of his life. The report can be brief and general where there are no problems. Specific details should be given where there is a problem, confusion, or doubt. Unusually strong emotional experiences often manifest material that we ought to lay before our spiritual director.

To Seek God's *Word Of Life* From The Host

"Man shall not live by bread alone, but by every word that proceeds from the mouth of God". (Mt 4:4) Early Christians did not have copies of the Bible. They heard portions of the "book of the Scriptures" read at the weekly Holy Eucharist. In addition to the scripture that they could memorize, they sought to find God's word in the "book of nature" and in the "book of the heart". They also listened for God's word coming to them through the lips of their spiritual elders.

In third century Egypt, it was common practice for a young seeker to approach one of the Fathers of the Desert with the request: "Father, give me a word of life." or "Father, give me a word to live by". At this request made in faith, the older monk would look into his heart for a specific word of instruction or encouragement fitted by the Holy Spirit (not merely by the elder himself) to the particular needs and possibilities of the petitioner. In our practice of spiritual direction, we will be blessed if we include this ancient belief and practice. Remember, we are not seeking a word of life *from* the spiritual director. Rather, we are seeking a word of life from God *through* the words spoken by the director.

God speaks His words of life to everyone in the sacred scriptures. For those who believe in sacramental spiritual direction, God speaks words of life to the individual person through the heart and lips of the elder. The Christian who believes this has a responsibility to give great weight to the words of the host. The host has nothing of his own to give, but God gives him a word of life for the visitor. Before the visitor and host meet, the visitor should be very intentional about receiving a word of life from God through the host. If, by the end of the meeting, the visitor is not sure he has heard "a word of life", he should explicitly ask for it from the host. Receiving by faith a "word of life" from God to you personally is one of the great blessings of spiritual direction.

To Receive Confirmation From The Host

Spiritual direction is a form of communion with God and is, therefore, prayer. As prayer, it enjoys the benefit the Lord Jesus promised to agreement in prayer. "Again I say to you, if two of you agree on earth about anything they ask, it will be done for them by my Father in heaven." (Mt. 18:19) The visitor presents herself, her life as a whole, to God in the sacrament of the spiritual director. She looks for the director's confirmation of her whole life in general and of her individual thoughts and actions in particular. The agreement of the elder signifies the agreement of God. How great a confirmation this agreement is to the visitor!

- *(1) General confirmation.* Implicitly always, and at certain times explicitly, the host who receives the intimate spiritual self-disclosure of the visiting Christian says: "Yes, you are God's beloved child. Yes, you are one with Jesus. You are living in His Spirit Who is empowering you to accomplish your mission in the world." The agreement of the two in this perception of faith is a powerful confirmation of the visiting Christian as a man or woman of God in the Spirit.

- *(2) Particular confirmation.* The visitor reveals to the host the most significant thoughts, actions, inspirations, and temptations of her daily life. She looks to him for confirmation, that is, agreement, that her own discernment of these things and her responses to them are according to the Holy Spirit. The visitor does not ask for permission. She looks for *agreement*. That agreement is particular confirmation.

A Note on disagreement in Spiritual Direction

If the spiritual director and visitor cannot agree, then the visitor has to reconsider the matter and make a decision. In this case, she will choose either to abandon her own opinion and *agree* with the host or, for her conscience's sake, to hold a different way of thinking or acting. The visitor has no obligation, other than her own conscientious choice, to submit to the opinions of the host. Neither does the host have any duty to convince the visitor, beyond expressing his or her disagreement. Disagreement can originate from honest error on the side of the visitor or on that of the host. Each one is responsible to God for their decision about this. Disagreement can also originate, not from error, but from the legitimate "range of freedom" given by God to each Christian in many areas of life. For instance, while adultery is not within the range of freedom, the decision to be a pacifist is. In matters that fall within the range of freedom, when the visitor and host choose different opinions, they meet in the agreement to honor each other's free choice.

To Receive Fraternal Correction

Our spiritual director host is our friend who is looking out for our best spiritual interests. She or he

Pathways to Union with Jesus

is our "corner man" who attends to our wounds and gives us advice in the spiritual boxing match we are engaged in. Our spiritual director is looking over our shoulder and from side to side, like a wary lioness protecting her cubs from the approach of any enemy.

We bring our host into our spiritual journey as a companion who will serve us like a guardian angel. The host's discernment, wisdom, experience, understanding, and prayers more than double ours alone… because Jesus adds His presence and His assent to our agreement.

A willingness to receive correction is an indispensable prerequisite for allowing God to protect and guide us through the spiritual director. We are to accept fraternal correction from our host by our own free choice and with clear-sighted vision. As we mature in the Christian life, it should be increasingly rare that our director feels it necessary to bring to our attention something that she feels is a moral fault or a spiritual error or danger. Instead, as we grow in the Spirit, our host will add her light to ours as we seek together the delicate nuances of God's perfect preferential will for us. Fraternal *correction* increasingly yields place to fraternal *confirmation*. Concern about personal *errors-to-be-corrected* decreases. Concern about personal *gifts-to-be-lived* increases.

In both cases, correction and confirmation, *a trusting willingness to be influenced (but not controlled) by our spiritual director is of absolute necessity.*

To Receive Spiritual Insight

Fraternal correction and confirmation refer to the activity of the moral will. Receiving insight from the host refers to the understanding mind. We begin our life in Christ from a place of darkness and ignorance of the things of God. After our enlightenment by initial saving faith, we gradually grow in understanding the implications of the revelation that has been granted to us. Prayerful spiritual study of the Sacred Scriptures is our chief external source of growth in understanding. Listening to other inspired Christians is another source. Among inspired Christians, our spiritual host holds a special place. Our spiritual director may not be smarter or know more than other commentators on the mystery of Christ. In terms of articulation, the things our host may say to us most probably have been spoken and written in better form elsewhere. But coming from the lips of our personal friend-spiritual director, these words are *for us personally, from God, here and now.*

Spiritual directors should generally avoid "teaching" during a spiritual direction meeting. If the host friend strongly feels that the visitor would be blessed by learning a certain relevant insight, let him or her humbly propose the idea. The visitor should receive the word offered in love and ponder it in her heart.

To Imitate The Host's Good Example

One of the reasons why we choose a particular person to be our elder is that we see in her or him some qualities of life that we would like for ourselves. Saint Athanasius wrote in his forth century classic, "Life of Anthony", that the young Anthony would go from one mature Christian to another to learn and imitate the virtues of each, the way a bee gathers nectar from many flowers.

Any mature Christian whom we might choose as our spiritual director is also a poor sinner whose only hope of eternal life is forgiveness through the shed Blood of Jesus. A Christian seeker will be blessed by God if he understands and forgives the limitations of his spiritual director's virtue. If there is a disappointing difference between our host's ideals and his reality, at least let us model ourselves on his good intentions and holy desires. As stated earlier, a person in whom we can find nothing to admire and nothing to imitate cannot be our spiritual elder.

Almost always, we can find *something* to admire! For example: Once I confessed a secret and humiliating sin to a certain young Christian. To my amazement, he then asked me to be his spiritual director. In spite of my unworthiness, he chose me because I was at least honest with him about my moral weakness.

To Hold The Host In A Special Love

The person who consents to be your spiritual director gives you a part of her life. She or he deserves a special place in your gratitude, love, and prayer. This love gets practical. If the host friend has need of material support for her life and ministry, the visitor should contribute something as his or her abundance allows. However, in my considered opinion and practice, no money should ever be required. If a directee feels led by the Spirit to give material support to the director, no exchange of money should take place at the meeting for spiritual direction. The host gives this service out of love without charging a fee. No visitor pays his host friend for hospitality! Many people are financially unable to contribute to the material support of their spiritual director. Those who are able to make contributions enable the director to serve those who cannot help her earn a living. By any criterion, spiritual direction is worth as much or more than any relationship of psychological counseling. However, unlike psychotherapy, I believe the meeting for spiritual direction should never be conceived as a "service for fee". It is beyond price! It is worth more than money. It is worth love and prayer from the heart of the receiver.

(3)   The Role Of The Host

To Give A Special Place In Love And Prayer For The Visitor

The director knows he or she has no power to make the visitor grow in the spiritual life. Therefore she is convinced that the most important thing she can contribute to that growth is to pray sincerely for the full realization of all that God desires to accomplish in the visitor's soul. The one who accepts to be director ought to care about the visitor's spiritual fulfillment as she cares for her own.

To be available for regularly scheduled and spontaneous meetings The host will practice a generous spiritual hospitality, giving priority to meeting with the visitor over other engagements that are less important in the sight of God.

To listen prayerfully and attentively to the confidences of the visitor

Since the host knows he cannot fix the problems of the visitor, he does not listen with a "helping" agenda. He just listens with loving attention to the words, meanings, and feelings revealed by the visitor. She simply lets the visitor's communication enter into her and have its effect on her. She does not screen the words for opportunities to correct errors or to ward off dangers. As a listening host, she renounces defensive or proactive attitudes and allows herself to be formed and informed by what the visitor communicates. The host believes and trusts that if she listens closely with love, God will fill her weakness and ignorance with divine strength and wisdom to empower and enlighten the visitor.

To Protect The Visitor From Unconscious Evil Thoughts

The must not be suspicious. Neither should he or she consciously sift everything the visiting brother or sister says seeking to find some evil thought lurking there. It will be given to her in the moment to know when to make a protective intervention in favor of the visitor. Her spirit, united with and inspired by the Holy Spirit, will disagree with something spoken by the visitor. With the uttermost gentleness and humility, she will point out what she believes falls short of the fullness of God's truth and love in the thought or deed revealed by the visitor. (Gal 6:1-5)

Not every imperfect thought or feeling should be judged and corrected. The director must know when the very act of verbal expression of the wrong idea or troublesome emotion is enough to correct it. The directee should feel safe with the host. The director should be the one person with whom a distraught visiting friend can express his or her hurt and anger –even though it be toward God— without fearing reproach or judgment. In this case, empathy, not correction, is the proper response of the director.

To show the compassion of God

Measured by God's call to perfect love, our fallen human nature is utterly ignorant, weak, and morally impure. We must acknowledge the brokenness of our lives before we can bring it to Jesus and ask for mercy and grace. Suffering is the fire ignited by our sins that God uses to purify us. More mature Christians have the privilege of more exquisite suffering by which they are yet further refined, from one degree of glory to another. All Christians are called to share in the suffering of Christ. From birth to death, all Christians are suffering.

While living in this world, the Christian's personal spirit already has eternal life in faith. But that is not enough. One who lives by faith has a fundamental, insatiable unmet need: to behold our Lord Jesus, face to face, in His Glory. No Christian can ever be satisfied until they attain this, the only ultimate happiness for which we were created. It may or may not be a conscious emotional feeling, but one's spirit ontologically thirsts for God. "As a deer pants for flowing streams, so pants my soul for you, O God. My soul thirsts for God, for the living God, When shall I come and appear before God." (Ps 42:1-2)

A wise spiritual director remains conscious of the immense suffering her visitor is always bearing—even though the visitor himself may not be thinking or speaking about it. A director cannot be too compassionate. God's act of saving the world is an act of Divine compassion. A spiritual director, serving as a sacramental person in the life of the directee, has more reason and responsibility than others to fulfill the universal law of Christ: "Be compassionate even as your Father is compassionate". (Lk 6:36)

To Have Absolute Faith In The Election And Perfection Of The Visitor

Despair is the most ominous of all temptations and the deadliest of all sins. Despair, in a variety of forms, presents itself repeatedly as a thought, attitude, or mood to all Christians during the course of their life journey. Of all of the demon wolves that attack the lambs of Christ, despair is the most cruel and devastating. Let the spiritual director decide beforehand never to lose confident hope, complete trust, and the assurance of faith concerning the salvation and full perfection of the Christian who comes for spiritual direction. To give up the least degree of that complete confidence would be a personal insult to Jesus Christ who was crucified for this brother and this sister. Never let that happen.

The host considers the visitor to be called to a beauty of perfection beyond any human being's wildest dreams. In faith, she confidently expects it to be realized, increasingly in time and perfectly in eternity. The whole sense and meaning of the companionship the host gives to the visiting friend is precisely this: Never doubting, to walk with her or him on the spiritual journey from one degree of glory to another, progressively approaching "the stature of the fullness of Christ". (Eph 4:13)

Pathways to Union with Jesus

To Speak Only And Always When The Holy Spirit Inspires

The ego-initiated words of the host must decrease. The words inspired by the Spirit must increase. Let the host pray for this gift. The more words the host volunteers, the more questionable becomes the origin of those words. Ours is a God of few words, even Only One, Jesus, the Eternal Word. "When words are many, transgression is not lacking" says the wise man (Pr. 10:19). No spiritual director will be perfect in his or her speech. Let the visiting friend be merciful in judgment on the host (like me!) who speaks too much.

To Utter The Prophetic Word Over The Visitor

When it is granted to the host to discern the gifts God is giving to the visitor, she will communicate this perception to the visiting friend. This testimony is a prophetic confirmation of the visitor's gifts and calling. The prophetic announcement acts like God-given rain and sunlight in spring, enabling these spiritual gifts of the visiting friend to blossom and bear fruit to the glory of God. This is true prophecy. The host speaks in the Name of God announcing beforehand her vision of the visitor's spiritual gifts of ministry, which later become manifest reality in the life of the visitor.

To Call The Visitor To Account

This should be a rare occurrence, but when the host is granted to see something amiss in the visitor's life, she ought to point it out. Humbly and gently she should make the visitor conscious of any unrecognized sins, prejudices, errors in moral judgment, misguided efforts, exaggerations, and pernicious religious misconceptions or anything else that presents an impediment or danger to the spiritual life of the visitor. If the visitor does not accept the correction, the spiritual director should not argue or become angry but privately redouble her prayer for the enlightenment of the beloved visitor.

To Encourage All That Is Good

The host should rejoice, and call the visiting friend to rejoice gratefully, over every grace and goodness God places in the heart, mind, and life of the visitor. The director encourages and blesses in prayer every holy desire the Christian visitor has for truth and love. Especially at those times when the visitor is passing through inner darkness and self-doubt, let the host call to mind the "big picture" of grace, election, blessing, and goodness in the visitor's life.

Ending The Relationship Of Spiritual Direction

A complete and perfect relationship between a visiting friend and host may be as brief as one meeting. Sometimes once is enough. Sometimes only one meeting is possible. On the other hand, a spiritual direction relationship may last until death. There are many legitimate reasons why the relationship may come to an end, such as illness, work, a change in residence, etc. These reasons are very common. They are immediately understandable and pose no danger to the broader and deeper love relationship between the two persons in Christ.

Spiritual direction should not be thought of the way we think of the physical relationships of marriage or family. The latter are exclusive and permanent relationships. Spiritual direction is an intentional relationship of an essentially temporary and provisional nature. The Spirit Who leads us to one person for spiritual companionship at one time in our lives may lead us to another at a later time. Christians have no objective obligation to visit exclusively with only one person for spiritual direction.

The spiritual direction relationship is initiated by one Christian who asks the other to serve as spiritual director. A seeker does so because she believes God will provide guidance and growth in the relationship. The time may arrive when she feels led by God to sit at the feet of someone else as her spiritual director. This is a perfectly normal spiritual development, provided the Christian is not frivolously pursuing a cult of 'more interesting' personalities. The Christian should not think she is being disloyal if, after a short or long time, she feels her spiritual life would grow in other complementary ways under the spiritual direction of someone else.

It is a very important duty of a spiritual director to remain non-possessive of the visiting friend. The intimacy of spiritual direction unites the two in a beautiful interpersonal love. The very authenticity of that love requires the host and the visitor to end their relationship when the greater spiritual good of the visitor indicates that she should seek spiritual direction from someone else.

The visiting friend's suggestion to end the relationship should not be construed by the host as implying any kind of criticism or personal rejection. The end of a spiritual direction relationship does not end their mutual love in Christ. The host can thank God that she has now completed the work of loving service to which God called her when she accepted to serve as spiritual host. The host may feel a certain emotional loss because she of her special affection for the Christian visitor. Now it is time for her love to be mature, like a good parent who blesses the child's departure from the family nest to enter upon adult pursuits. She should encourage the visiting Christian to make this change of spiritual direction in prayerful hope for the many new spiritual benefits the visiting friend will receive by walking with a different director.

The love between the visiting Christian and the host Christian does not come to an end. What they have shared in spiritual direction is precious and is recorded forever in heaven. When the time of relating in spiritual direction is over the former host must completely abandon the role of spiritual director. They let each other go from their passing roles in spiritual direction, in order to hold each other in their original and ultimate relationship: Friends in Christ.

Pathways to Union with Jesus

The spiritual lives of many baptized Christians are comatose and some are moribund. Such people are not engaged in a serious spiritual direction relationship. By contrast, in almost every case, Christians who do engage in a theologically sound practice of spiritual direction are live rich, full, maturing lives in Christ. Having the loving companionship of a spiritual friend on the inner journey is a precious pathway to union with Jesus.

TO THE PATHWAY OF LIFE

We have studied four of the great spiritual Pathways to Union with Jesus: Lectio Divina, The Jesus Prayer, Discernment of Thoughts, and Spiritual Direction. These classical devotions purify the heart. Purity of heart enables our faith to see Jesus dwelling within our hearts. Seeing Jesus by faith and union with Him in love transforms us in His likeness. These disciplines are tried and proven devotional pathways, but they lead to a greater pathway: life itself.

We engage in physical exercise so that our heart and muscles will be strong not just during the time we spend in the gym but in all of our lives. Similarly, the diligent consistent practice of the spiritual disciplines we have studied empowers us to live in union with Jesus at every moment of our lives. In the next and final chapter, we will explore how we can experience transforming union with Jesus at all times in The Pathway of Life.

CHAPTER SIX

THE PATHWAY OF LIFE

THE PATHWAY OF LIFE

"For me to live is Christ." (Phil 1:21)

The formal practices of spiritual disciplines presented in the preceding pages are intended to give beginners a place to start. (And aren't we all beginners?) As we advance, we do not jettison the disciplines. Rather, they grow into the fabric of our entire life. We practice times dedicated to lectio divina, but we also remember and recite scripture passages frequently during the day. The time we spend in the formal practice of the Jesus Prayer extends into a habit of calling upon the Lord in love continually during the day and night. Conscious intentional discernment of our thoughts becomes a subliminal vigilance that springs into action when we are tempted or troubled as we make our way through the day. We continue to have formal visits with an elder for spiritual direction, but we find ourselves spontaneously opening our hearts to share the good and the bad with mature Christian friends with whom we fellowship in our daily lives. The spiritual disciplines become our spiritual way of life.

There are two simultaneous, complimentary, inseparable ways in which our entire lives become authentic pathways to union with Jesus: our faith

Pathways to Union with Jesus

and our love. A believer, and only a believer, loves with agape love given by the Holy Spirit. A person can love with agape love only if she or he is one who believes. Loving faith is a permanent quality always present in a Christian. The gift of faith in Jesus requires and empowers us to bring every moment and every event in our daily lives into the light of God's love revealed to us in Jesus. The gift of agape-love for Jesus enables us to love Him in all people and in the entire creation given to Him by the Father.

Faith: Knowing Jesus In All Of Life

By faith I mean our acceptance of Jesus Christ as the Light of revelation given to us by God the Father through the Holy Spirit. Once we are illumined by the Light of the world, we must bring all of our human experience into this new Light of Christ. By reinterpreting all things in the Light of Christ we can find union with Him in the entire pathway of our lives. From the moment of our rebirth in Christ, the Spirit works in our spirit to change the way we think about everything: God, ourselves, other people, the whole of creation, and every event that happens in our lives. This is what St Paul means when he tells us we have the mind of Christ. (1Cor 2:16) In a life-long process we repudiate the mind of darkness and put on the mind of Christ.

The Mind of Darkness

Before we came into our new Life in Christ, we had been born and bred in a dark fallen world. In our experience, this world was sometimes a place of sweet goodness and it other times it was bitterly evil. We felt joy when we saw life bursting forth on every side, only to have our joy dampened and our hopes disappointed when we saw death put an end to every living being, even the ones we most loved.

During that pre-Christian time in our lives, Mother Nature at first seemed kind to us and supremely beautiful. Then we learned by painful experience that she can also be cruel, unpredictable, and unspeakably ugly. The sky above blessed us with the glorious light of the sun and cursed us with storms, meteors, draught, and floods. The more we learned, the more we realized we are under attack at all times. From birth onward we endured and survived the death-dealing chaos of natural disasters and invisible viruses and microbes that would kill us. Perhaps worst of all, we came to realize that we human beings exploit, harm, and kill one another. Each person and each people group competes with

Pathways to Union with Jesus

the others for power and possessions. We saw the 'civilized war' of ruthless competition and we saw the barbaric horrors of World War. What had been rarely seen heinous acts of terrorism became every day atrocities.

Naturally, we learned to view this world as an extremely dangerous place. Bad things could happen to us at any time. We saw ruined lives like undead carcasses strewn along the highways and byways of our lives…victims of disease, accident, and violence. Others were taken down by alcohol, drugs, criminal prosecution, and mental breakdown. So many others put an end to their misery by suicide. If there were no hope for a blessed eternity, this world would qualify as hell.

To survive in the hostile jungle of this world, we learned to defend and protect ourselves. Sometimes we trampled others in our competitive rush to avoid bad things or to get something good out of this life. Raw experience had taught us that we could not just defenselessly let life happen to us. We had to on guard, always ready to fight or to flee at the approach of bad things at any time.

Living like that for so long, we formed deep mental and emotional habits and attitudes of uncertainty, distrust, suspicion, fear, disgust, and a profound conviction that we cannot trust what might happen to us. We could not rest. We were permanently engaged in defensive or offensive battle. Seemingly abandoned by an unknown God to this hateful ordeal, what could we think about God, about ourselves, and about our personal value?

If we want our whole lives to become a Pathway to union with Jesus, we have to abandon these former perceptions and attitudes regarding God and our life in the world. We have to replace our old mind of darkness with the new mind of Christ that has been revealed to us. We do this by intentionally reinterpreting all things, good and evil, in the Light of Christ.

Reinterpretation Of All Things Good

Every good thing we experience, be it as small as a cool breeze on a hot day or as momentous as the birth of a child, is a sign and a seed-promise of the perfect eternal happiness that God wills to give to all who are willing to receive. Jesus, the Light of the world shows us that every creature is created good by God and all nature will be freed from its bondage to chaos and decay. Every creature will share, according to the nature of each one, in the glorious eternal life of the children of God. Sparrows do not fall to the earth in this life without the permission of their Creator. The Creator of all things gave them being and life. God's pleasure and His glory is the fullness of being and life of all of His creatures. Sin brought death into creation. When the Lord Jesus returns to make all things new, no sparrow will ever fall again, because in the new creation harm and death shall be no more forever. Until then, every finite good thing we experience in this mortal life is a foretaste and a promise of the infinite goodness that will be manifest to us and in us in the Eternal Life to come.

Reinterpretation Of All Things Evil

Many of the same evil things that happened to us before we were reborn in Christ still happen to us after our rebirth. Christians suffer all of the material afflictions that happen to all human beings and they die in the flesh, just like everybody else. The Light of Christ shows us that God suffers our suffering. God subjects Himself to the things we suffer. God is nothing but compassionate Love. We are His beloved children. God suffers the pain of every person.

Does God cause our suffering in order to bring about our glory? Absolutely NO! God does not do evil to achieve a good purpose! Human sin is the exclusive cause of all suffering and death. If sin is the root cause of all suffering in nature and in human life, why does a loving God allow us to sin? Because His love for us prevents Him from destroying the freedom that makes us persons. If God did not give us freedom to sin, we would not have the freedom to love.

Sin ends in death. Death is the annihilation of the person in temporal life. End of story. Until God writes the epilogue to our human story by taking our sin, suffering, and death upon Himself and adds a divine sequel: resurrection to blessed eternal life.

Here is a summary statement of the Father's eternal plan to end sin, suffering, and death: God in Jesus revealed His forgiving love for us by taking all of our sin, suffering, and death upon Himself on the cross. By raising Jesus to eternal life in the Body, God revealed His Life-giving and glorifying love for us. Now, and for the remainder of human history, God continues to reveal His immeasurably great love for us in Person of Jesus Christ. This love of Christ overwhelms us. God's love revealed in Jesus draws us out of our fear-driven sinful selfish love. As we experience the ineffable blessedness of being God's chosen beloved in Jesus and find ourselves filled with His grace and made alive by the Spirit of His resurrection, we freely choose to love. Love puts an end to the sin that is the ultimate cause of all suffering and death.

In what way does Jesus change our suffering and death into something ineffably good and beautiful? Our Lord expressed His love for us sinners by choosing to be one with us in our sin, suffering, and death. In love, He offered His passion and death as a sacrificial prayer for our redemption. At the same time, Jesus' suffering unto death on the cross was a supreme expression of filial obedient love for His Eternal Father. In all, Jesus has infused into human suffering unto death the meaning of divine love. That is ineffably good and beautiful!

Having risen with Jesus and now living in Him, our sufferings coalesce with His. We no longer live, love, suffer, and die alone, but Christ is in us and we in Him. In our personal temporal suffering and death, Jesus continues to express ineffable divine love as we accept our share in His sufferings and offer them as a sacrificial prayer of compassionate love for sinners and obedient filial love for our Father. That, too, is ineffably good and beautiful!

Embracing Your Worthiness

From the beginning of your existence in the womb, you did not know the God who breathes you forth into being. You did not know that God loved you and chose you before the world existed. You were born not knowing that God rejoiced and all the angels with Him at your birth. Father God delighted at the moment of your conception, because the time He long-desired had fully come. In that eternally planned moment, at the appointed time, the Father expressed Himself anew: He breathed you into existence. God spoke and you came into real existence in time out of mere possibility in His Eternity. On that blessed day, God's spoken word, the created word of God that you are, came into existence in your mothers womb.

But you were born in the darkness of original sin, born into a sinful world of darkness. In that darkness you were bred. From your conception, you knew nothing of God and nothing of your true self. You, like every child at conception, began to record your experiences in this world –a world they later told you was "natural". From the sum total of all of your experiences in the darkness, you formed a false notion of who you are and what you are worth. Unintentionally, you fashioned in your mind a distorted image of who you really are. That is, not knowing yourself as a unique expression of God's Life, you formed a self-concept from what you were told by other ignorant people, by the bad things that happened to you in this world of darkness, by the hateful lies of demons, and by your own self-denigrating thoughts. There we all were, every one of us, lost in the God-less world, trapped in inner darkness, walking in pain and sorrow through the outer world of darkness, threatened and demeaned by its countless dangers, wounds, and insults. We had no idea of who we really are or what we are truly worth.

Then came the Blessed Light!

The Blessed Light of Life first came into this dark world many years ago in the Middle East. Since His resurrection, Jesus has become the Light Who enlightens every willing person. You are willing. You believe in Jesus. You have already come into the Light. In your spirit, you have been transferred from the kingdom of darkness into His marvelous Light. Since your first enlightenment, your mind, with all of its untrue information, wrong attitudes, misunderstandings, errors, and ignorance, is being enlightened and transformed by the grace of the Spirit. You are progressively making your own the mind of Christ. You must want it. You have to choose to think of yourself, other people, and the whole world in the Light of Christ.

If we desire to find union with Jesus in the pathway of our life, we absolutely must allow the Light Who dwells in our personal spirit to illumine the thoughts of our mind about our true identity as beloved child of the Father and uniquely precious friend of Jesus. In His gracious love for you, God invites and empowers you to become unceasingly aware of your life in Jesus and His Life in you.

Worthiness means worth-full-ness. There are no words adequate to describe how full of worth you are precisely in the unique person you are. Let's reflect upon your worth. God is not content to be God without you. As long as God has existed in eternity He desired you, loved you, planned your eternal beatitude with Him in glory. You are an incomparable delight to the heart of God.

God would have shown you an immeasurably great love if He had intended to give you a blessed human life in His Presence forever in eternity. He intends to give you infinitely more. In His love for you, God has determined to take you above and beyond your natural condition as a human being. He decided, from all eternity, to take you into the inner Life of the Trinity. God has united you to His Eternal Son, incarnate in the Person of Jesus. You are one with Jesus as Jesus is one with the Father in the Spirit. I appeal to you in the Name of God: Believe and receive the inexpressible Gift of God that makes you a partaker of the divine nature. You now live by faith what you will live by sight: You are in Jesus the beloved Child of God in whom God the Father takes His delight.

What, then, are you worth! You are of such worth that the Eternal Word abandoned His divine glory in the Bosom of Father God and took on the humiliation of a mortal human body in this hellish world of darkness. He did it to get you for Himself, because He loves you so much! The Father gave up His Son, His only Son in whom He delights, to blasphemous insult, rejection by all, cruel torture, and a shameful excruciating death on the cross in place of you the sinner. The Risen Son gave you the Holy Spirit Who raised Him from the dead to raise you up to new Life in Jesus. It is no longer you who live but the Risen Christ is living in you.

You must disregard every condemning word from within your own mind or from the outside world. Your sins and limitations have no impact on your worth to God – worth which never was based on your behavior. You, sinner, must live by faith in the Son of God Who loves you and gave Himself to death on the cross for you personally.

You are God the Father's gift to God the Son Incarnate. You are an expression like no other of the Father's love for the Son. You are a unique manifestation of the glory of God. You are God's gift to men and to angels. You make every created spirit know God and Jesus in a unique way. No one can know God the way you make God known except by knowing you. You are necessary for the fullest possible happiness of all God's elect. You are indispensable and irreplaceable for the fullness of the Body of Christ. Jesus is glorified in you. Just knowing you gives incomparable joy to God, to Jesus, and to all angels and saints. Because you are beloved of the Father and clothed in the glory of Jesus in a personally unique manner, you do not have to do anything. Just be there for others to know and love you! Your most generous gift of love for God's holy ones consists in simply giving them the blessed joy of knowing you.

If you know these things in your spirit by faith, blessed are you if you think them in your mind, the mind of Christ!

Love: Loving Jesus In All Of Life

Christ is God incarnate. All things are originally created and continue in existence by, through, for, and in Christ. Jesus is in all things as the Father's Eternal Word spoken in the creation, preservation, and redemption of all things. In the Spirit, Jesus is in all who believe.

Love has been poured into our hearts by the Holy Spirit: Love for Jesus our Divine Savior; love for God His Father and our Father; love for every human being beloved by God; love for the whole material creation of God.

Agape-love is a continuous unwavering state of being of the person who loves. The inner state of love is the permanent reality that produces the fleeting actions that express our love in the outer world. Love is born when a personal spirit knows good. "No one is good except God alone" says the Lord. (Mk 10:18) He goes on to mark out good deeds. Good deeds, good people, good things, and the Good Jesus, all participate in and manifest the only Good God, each in its own way and degree with Jesus being the very incarnation of the Whole Goodness of God.

While we seek to know God and all things in the light of Christ, we ought also to seek to love God and all created things in the love of Christ. For our whole life to become a pathway to union with Him, we must seek to love, always, everywhere, and everyone. Loving must become our living. We should hunger in prayer for agape-love because it is a gift of the Spirit before it is our life. No mere passing action, agape-love is a permanent, every deepening state of being of those who know the Lord.

We have been sent into this world to love the persons God places in our lives. The Father first draws us to Jesus. Jesus sends us to love those to whom He sends us. We are present to Jesus by *intentional* love for Him in all we do and suffer on our mission to be *present* and *compassionate* to the persons to whom He sends us. Let us consider…

BEING INTENTIONAL. Agape-love is a fire in the heart that never goes out. Our life in time is successive, one moment, one action, after another. We ought to make an intention, once and for all, to dedicate our whole lives to the glory of God, for Him to use all during our time in this world. Our hearts will beat of themselves without intention. Let's be intentional: dedicate our every heartbeat to the glory of God. We will breathe mechanically and automatically, willing or not. Let us intentionally consecrate our every breath to the honor, glory, and service of Christ our God. In our quest for union with Jesus, for love of Him, let us dedicate to God every movement of our body, every pain and pleasure, every emotion, every word and every deed, every joy and every sorrow. All for Jesus! What else should we live for? All for God in Jesus. Nothing for anything else. "Whatever you do in word or deed, do everything in the name of the Lord Jesus, giving thanks to God the Father through him." (Co, 3:17)

BEING PRESENT. It is a common tragedy that we do not notice what is most obvious and we overlook what is most important. Here is the greatest of all good things in life, the highest personal fulfillment, and greatest happiness possible on earth: (1) To be present to Jesus in the unitive prayer of mutual knowing and loving; and (2) to be present to the persons to whom we are sent, mutually knowing, valuing, and loving each other as God knows, values, and loves each one. This is how we love God Whom we have not seen by loving our companion whom we do see. (cf. 1Jn 4: 20) We will never do anything in our lives more significant that this: Being present to Jesus and to other persons in mutual faith and loving attention.

BEING COMPASSIONATE. Consider the condition of all human beings in the whole world. All are sinners. All are suffering. Every person we meet every day is struggling with evil from inner brokenness and outer troubles. All are going through difficulties, trials, heartaches, and disappointments. All are burdened with awareness of their moral failures. Every person you see is assailed by feelings of inadequacy, guilt, and shame.

Jesus shows us in His own life the compassion of God the Father. He tells us to be compassionate as our heavenly Father is compassionate. Therefore, we will be united with Jesus on the pathway of life to the extent that we become increasingly compassionate, universally compassionate, to every human being, never condemning any person no matter how heinous their evil deeds. In compassion pray for *all* human beings to be found and saved by the Good Shepherd. By a life of compassion we are in this world as He is in heaven.

When we encounter or just hear about people who do very bad things or when we meet people suffering evil things along our pathway they should awaken our compassion, our prayer, and our hunger for Christ Who is our only hope for an end to all of the sins and afflictions of every suffering human being.

Walking In Faith And Love

Walking in faith and love enables us to be united with Jesus in our mind and heart –never perfectly, but ever increasingly. Union with Jesus forms new attitudes in us toward our experiences in the pathway of our life.

Walking in Grace

By faith we have received the total unconditional love of God. We are beloved by God's choice. His personal love for us comes from His grace, not from our behavior. We can ignore and silence every voice from within or from without that suggests that we are not good enough to be completely beloved by God just as we are. The inner tormenting struggle for self-worth is completely over. Forever!

Walking in Gratefulness

We are like the ten lepers who met Jesus. He told us to go show ourselves to the priests. Walking along, we suddenly became aware that we are healed. Nine walk away with no thought for the One Who healed them. We must be the tenth leper who returns to Jesus, falling at His feet praising God and giving thanks. Sisters and Brothers, the toils, tears and tortures of this life are endless. Jesus delivers us from them all. We can rest in Him Who has made all things well. Every tear will be wiped away. Not one of our hairs will be lost. Sin, hopeless suffering, and death have been destroyed forever on His cross. We can walk through the fleeting specters of disaster that stalk us in this passing world because we have received an eternal treasure that can never be taken from us. Therefore, let us continually offer to God a thanksgiving sacrifice, a heart that pronounces the Name of Jesus in gratefulness.

Walking in the Power of Providence

When we lived in the darkness, we had no idea what to expect in the course of our lives, good or evil. We did not know if we would have the ability to accomplish the goals and the strength endure the hardships our life would require. We lived in uncertainty, doing our best and hoping things would turn out all right.

Now living in the Light, we know that the whole course of our lives at every moment is under the loving control of God's power and providence. God planned all of our days and all of our actions before we were born. He foresaw all of the bad things that we would do and all the bad things that would happen to us...

and He worked out a plan to make all of it, everything, work together for our good. All of the uncertainties of our life in this world are under the certain control of God's providence, a providence designed to make us perfect through suffering in this temporal life leading to eternal beatific glory in the Life to come.

From the moment we were raised to life in the Risen Christ by grace we were sent on a mission into the world. (Jn 17:18; 20:21) We have the power of God to succeed in our lives and to complete the mission entrusted to us. We remain vulnerable to circumstances over which we have no control. We can still be wounded, even tragically wounded, by the free choices of the people to whom we are sent. By faith we know that, no matter what happens to us, God will strengthen us to come through every trial with greater love. Each of us is a word spoken by God into the world. None of us will return to Him empty but will accomplish all that He sent us to do. Amen!

Walking in Joy

The Lord Jesus was sorrowful unto death in the garden of Gethsemane. (Mk 14:34) Paul experienced "great sorrow and unceasing anguish". (Rm 9:2) He was "so utterly burdened beyond our strength that we despaired of life itself." (2Cor 1:8) Peter esteems it a gracious thing when "mindful of God, one endures sorrows while suffering unjustly." (1Pt 2:19) James advises suffering Christians: "Is anyone among you suffering? Let him pray." (Js 5:13) With these biblical testimonies, the witness of our own experience, and what we have painfully seen in the lives of Christians around us, it is incontrovertible that suffering and sorrow are integral parts of the Christian life.

Yet joy prevails. Even in the midst of our suffering and our sorrow, our trust in God's promise to make all things right in eternity gives us a spiritual joy that no earthly sorrow can take from us. Jesus wants His joy to be in us and our joy to be full. (Jn 15: 11) He even prayed to the Father that His joy would be made perfect in us. (Jn 17:13) He promised us that "your hearts will rejoice, and no one will take your joy from you." (Jn 16:22). The perfect permanent joy of Jesus is ours because we have His total unconditional love forever.

Our spiritual joy does not eliminate the suffering we experience during our mission in Christ through the world but it strengthens and comforts us in our sorrow. There is a selfish deadly sorrow that comes from not trusting in the love, power, and promise we have from God. We give no place to these sorrows of unbelief. But the sorrow that comes to us as our

Pathways to Union with Jesus

sharing in the cup of His suffering is precious holy sorrow. It is the right, good, and beautiful sorrow of compassionate love. Paradoxically, with Paul we can rejoice in our sufferings as a participation in the suffering of Christ. (cf. Col 1:24) Indeed, blessed and happy are we who morn until we are comforted by the coming of the Lord. (cf. Mt 5: 4)

We walk in the joy of union with God in Jesus. We have been made one with Jesus, the Beloved Son of God, crucified in time past and now risen and glorified in eternity. He is the Vine. We are the branches. Even during this temporal human life we share in the joy of Jesus in His glorified risen Life with the Father.

As we make our way on the pathway of life, we will experience the great joy of moments of conscious awareness of the immeasurable love God the Father has for us in Jesus. The Father's love is in us always, eternally. But for our joy on our journey through time, He continually visits us with moments of heightened conscious awareness of His love, making us cry out in delight, "Abba, Father".

We walk in the joy of immediate access to God the Father through His Son. Jesus went to the Father in eternity when He ascended into heaven. Jesus is in the Presence of the Father always. We are in Jesus, as members of His one living Body. That means we, in Him, are always in the Presence of the Father in our personal spirit. Our personal spirits "are hid with Christ in God" the Father. (Col 3:3) At every moment of our conscious life in this world of time we always have the invitation to the immediate personal Presence of both Jesus and the Father. God the Son and God the Father, One in God the Spirit, dwell together in our hearts. In a single breath, in a heartbeat, at any time, we can speak to God in personal conversation as to One Who loves us. We are very foolish, like a man starving while seated at a sumptuous banquet table, if we do not satisfy our hungry hearts by continual loving communion with God Who is always with us for our joy.

Finally, I hold up for your contemplation the greatest of all joys we can experience on the Pathway of Life. Jesus comes to us and manifests Himself to us. He reveals Himself to us in our hearts. He shows Himself to us as our Friend who delights in us and enjoys our company. What incomparable joy it is to behold the Lord Jesus in our vision of faith, abiding in our hearts, loving us individually, personally, with the love of delight!

When I see Jesus enjoying supreme delight in me, as the person I am, I am overwhelmed by grateful joy beyond all comprehension. This is the joy of fulfillment for which St Paul prays to the Father on behalf of his friends in Ephesus:

> "that according to the riches of his glory
> he may grant you
> to be strengthened with power through his Spirit in your inner
> being, that Christ may dwell in your hearts through faith;
> that rooted and grounded in love, you may have power to comprehend…
> the breadth and length and height and depth,
> and to know the love of Christ which surpasses knowledge, that
> you may be filled with all the fullness of God" (Eph 3:16-19)

Dear Ones of Christ who read these words, I pray that your practice of the spiritual pathways may purify your heart so that you may see God and know His Love more and more, and that all of life may become your Pathway to Union with Jesus.

Milton Keynes UK
Ingram Content Group UK Ltd.
UKHW020328031224
451863UK00012B/445